50 BEST DOG WALKS / HIKES

Around VICTORIA

AND

SOUTHEASTERN VANCOUVER ISLAND

By

Leo Buijs

Dedicated to my son's dog Anore

"She was always so happy to see me when I got home from work, you will be missed."
Joost Buijs

Printed in Canada

Second edition

National Library of Canada Cataloguing in Publication

Buijs, Leo, 1946-
      50 best dog walks/hikes around Victoria and southeastern Vancouver Island / Leo Buijs. -- 2nd ed.

Includes index.
ISBN 0-9735527-0-0

      1. Dog walking--British Columbia--Victoria--Guidebooks. 2. Dog walking--British Columbia--Vancouver Island--Guidebooks. 3. Victoria (B.C.)--Guidebooks. 4. Vancouver Island (B.C.)--Guidebooks. I. Title. II. Title: Fifty best dog walks/hikes around Victoria and southeastern Vancouver Island.

FC3844.2.B83 2004   917.11'28044   C2004-902643-7

This book is published by Seaview Investments Ltd.,
2705 Seaview Road, Victoria BC V8N 1K7 Canada

E-mail   seaview@pacificcoast.net
Web site www.pacificcoast.net/~seaview/

🐾 🐾 🐾 🐾 🐾 🐾 🐾 🐾 🐾 🐾 🐾 🐾 🐾 🐾 🐾 🐾 🐾 🐾 🐾 🐾 🐾 🐾 🐾 🐾

50 BEST DOG WALKS/HIKES

AROUND VICTORIA
AND
SOUTHEASTERN VANCOUVER ISLAND

CONTENTS

Introduction

Why another walking/hiking book for Victoria and Southeastern Vancouver Island?

Most hiking books that are on the market today are either for serious backcountry hiking or cover easier family hikes in parks that are often not accessible for dogs. Besides this, there have been many changes recently in park and beach regulations pertaining canines. Some of these regulations have become stricter. Others are loosening up in ways that allow dogs off-leash at times or in certain areas.

For many dog owners this has become very confusing and on top of that, many parks now charge parking fees. This guide is an honest attempt to clarify the current status of the best 50 dog-walks or hikes around Victoria and Southeastern Vancouver Island, regardless of whether they are in public parks or elsewhere. My descriptions list all the pros and cons, including any parking or admission fees and restrictions for dogs. Therefore, this guide can be a helpful planning tool for locals, travelers and tourists in this area that like to take their dog to places where they are welcome.

This guidebook deals mostly with easy to moderate level walking/hiking in urban and country settings, beaches and parks where our lovable canines are always welcome one way or another.

What to expect in this book

I have tried to make this book as practical as possible. Besides "to-the-point" description of the best 50 dog walks/hikes around Victoria and Southeastern part of Vancouver Island, this guidebook also covers safety and behavioral aspects as well as hints on car travel with 'Fido.'

The 50 walks/hikes are divided in five logical regions. The first region, marked with a **V** are all in or around Greater Victoria. The second group, marked **P** for Peninsula, covers walks/hikes on or near the Saanich Peninsula. Next is the Western section, marked **W**, located between Victoria and Port Renfrew. The following region, marked **D** for Duncan, are hikes north of the Malahat and around the Duncan area. Last but not least, are the hikes marked **N** for Nanaimo, covering that area and up to Parksville and Qualicum Beach.
A sub-classification of the "10 Best of the Best" are listed in the back of the guide. You will also find there a listing of the "Best Beaches" to run your dog and the "Best Swimming Holes."

Criteria that were used to derive the Best 50 Dog Walks/Hikes and 'overall' rating

Everyone has their own interpretation or model for the 'best' of any kind. In regards to dog-walking/hiking, I have tried to put the dog central and make the owner secondary as to what he or she might find important. Factors/criteria I used in evaluation were:

1. Accessibility for the dog and owner
2. Variety of terrain
3. 'Bonus point' for drinking water available or coffee shop/restaurant nearby that caters to your pet's needs
4. Swimming for the dog
5. Scenery
6. Botanical or historical interest
7. Rustic or urban setting

Bone, 🦴 from one to five 🦴🦴🦴🦴 will indicate how good the overall rating is according to Jazz and me.

Trail and hike rating according to difficulty

One paw, 🐾 meaning **easy**, mostly flat or level terrain, suitable for all abilities or ages.

🐾 🐾 Two paws rating is **moderate,** the trail may have uneven parts, some steep sections and is therefore more arduous.

🐾 🐾 🐾 Three paws means **challenging**. This could be uneven/ narrow, with steep or slippery sections only suitable for more experienced hikers and dogs.

Trail Condition rating

☺ A well maintained smooth trail with blacktop, gravel, or bark mulch and with few rocks or roots, reasonably even.

☺ A regularly used and maintained trail but with small hurdles such as roots, rocks, maybe a creek to cross, not always an even surface.

☹ Difficult and irregular surface, narrow or poorly marked trail that is only maintained by use, or the lack of it.

Maps and directions

I have included maps to locate the hike's access points, and recommended direction of the walk/hike. These maps are not always to scale and should not be used for navigation.

The last paragraph in each of the 50 Best Walks/ Hikes always has 'Directions to get there.' An approximate driving distance or time by car is indicated by 🚗 and measured from downtown Victoria, Nanaimo, Duncan or ferry terminals.

3

Good news for dogs and owners alike in the City of Victoria

By the time this second edition is published, the City of Victoria hopefully will have implemented the nine (9) new 'leash optional' parks. **See page 7 for map.** They are: Arbutus, # 2 on map

Vic West, # 50	Topaz, # 49
Oswald, # 33	Oaklands, # 32
Redfern, # 41	Pemberton, # 34
Central, # 12	Fisherman's Wharf, # 19

The nine city parks will be a welcome alternative to the one and only official 'off leash' park that the City of Victoria has at time of writing. However, they are small city parks, great for playing and off-leash running, but do not offer additional hiking opportunities. What it does mean is, that Victoria dog-owners and visitors will have better opportunities for running their dog and that the **Dallas Road Off-leash** area will become less busy. That is great news for anyone that will take their dog on the **Clover Point to Ogden Point** (see V2) walk.

Disclaimer

Please note that I cannot be held responsible for any discrepancies, inaccuracies, or omissions in this guidebook.

Walks, hikes and beaches shown and recommended in this book may be off limits to dogs at times due to change in park regulations or conditions. Hikers will always travel at their own risk and it is the individuals own responsibility to check for changes by being observant of signs posted at parks and beaches or by asking the appropriate authorities, officials or local residents.

In relation to walk/hike ratings and trail conditions, each dog owner is responsible for their own well being. You should always evaluate conditions for yourself and your dog and not rely on my ratings since everyone's condition is different from another and every dog is different from my dog.

Updates

Thriving to keep this guide up to date, I appreciate any comments or recommendations from readers. Please send me your comments by e-mail only, to seaview@pacificcoast.net . In return, I will inform you when updates or revisions will be available. Just send me an e-mail with 'update Dog Hike' in the subject-line and you will receive notification by e-mail when updates come available

Scratch a Dog

Scratch a dog and you'll find a permanent job.

Franklin P. Jones.

Is your dog ready for hiking?

This chapter is about preparing your dog for a hike and since this is not your ordinary walk around the block, you need to make sure that you have at least the basics in order.

- We need a good collar, one that fits snugly but not to tightly. A flat hand should be easy to slide under the collar. If there is too much room, adjust it so it would not come off in any situation.
- A good quality leash is next. Leather is beautiful, long lasting but not practical if it gets wet often. Nylon is as strong and dries quickly.
- Identification tag well attached to the collar.
- Let's make your dog stand out. A bandana tied to its collar can help identify your dog from a distance.
- We need lots of water. Eight ounces for every hour hiking. But who is to carry the load?
- Consider a backpack, either one for yourself or one that can be attached as a dog-pack on the shoulders of your dog.

- A small first aid kit including
  - topical disinfecting cream
  - tweezers and small scissors
  - some sealed bandages
  - tape and duct-tape
  - gauze and 4" square gauze pads
  - Vaseline or petroleum jelly, to cover ticks or tick powder/spray
  - Hydrocortisone spray (for stings, rashes)
  - Peroxide 3% and painkiller
  - bug repellant

- A cell-phone might come in handy, or at least bring your veterinarian's phone number.
- In snowy winter conditions, I believe there might be good use for dog-booties. They avoid ice-balls forming between the toe pads and provide warmth.

Folks Will Know
Folks will know how large your soul is
By the way, you treat a dog.
Charles F. Durhan

More information on Dog-Packs.

Before we took Jazz, our golden retriever who is featured on the cover of this guidebook, hiking, she had done a lot of sailing and got used to wearing a life-jacket very easily. Dog packs sit almost the same way as life-jacket and are measured the same way. As long as you let the dog get used to it beforehand, she will be fine.
To determine the size of pack for your dog, measure the girth of the rib cage. The pack should fit snug and secure without limiting the walk of the dog.

A good dog pack has storage pouches on both sides. It should sit as high to the shoulders as possible. The straps should be situated where they will not chafe.
Do not expect your dog to carry a heavy load. Get him or her used to it by just attaching the pack. After a while, try stuffing the pack with light things. A smart way to make the dog look forward to wearing the pack is putting some treats in. Every time you take some out, Max will associate the treats with the pack and the hiking.
The load you can put in the pack depends on the size and weight of your dog. Generally, a healthy dog can easy carry about 25 to 33 percent of its body weight.
Never put anything breakable in there. If your dog is anything like ours, the minute it smells a nice grassy field, she goes down and rolls enjoyably on her back for a while. If your dog has any kind of hip-dysplasia, forget it. Consult your veterinarian if you suspect your dog might have back problems before you buy any type of dog-pack.

A good dog-pack has storage pouches on both sides

City of Victoria new 'leash optional' parks (read page 4)

Let's take that dog for a hike

You have been looking through this guide, found a few hikes that are close to your place and want to take advantage of the nice weather you have right now. Before you put on the dog's collar and get the car fired up, let's have a look at a few important aspects to make this hiking with your dog a success.

Is your dog up to it?
Hiking is a fantastic way of preventing some physical and behavioral problems. Just as with humans, a large number of dogs are suffering from overweight. Obviously, running with you up trails and beaches, jumping in lakes and ocean surely is a great way of taking these extra pounds off, while healthy dogs will maintain their good condition longer. The exercise from the hike will avoid destructive habits simply by change of scenery and tiredness while you as dog owner will get a better owner/dog relationship.

Is your dog of the right breed?
While most dogs love to go out with their bosses, not all dogs are suited to substantial hikes. How long you like to make the hike depends on the size and character of your dog or hound. Working dogs like Malamutes or Shepherds, hounds like the Greyhound, and sporting dogs such as Spaniels, and Retrievers can easily endure longer hikes.
If you haven't chosen your hiking companion, keep in mind what sort of hiking you would like to do and take your pick accordingly.

Train your dog before that big hike.
Just as we humans need to train for a 10 K run, so does your four-legged companion, even if it is just for a two to three hour hike. Depending on the activity level of your dog, you should try a few easy hikes before you decide to take the dog on that big one.

Behavior
Make sure that you are always in control of your dog. If you are hiking and suddenly run into a situation where you have to restrain your dog,

you should be able to do so. Wildlife, a horseback rider or a group of small children can be a great distraction to your roaming friend and the quicker you have this situation under control the better.

Better still, keep your dog at close range or leashed. Do not give other people a chance to complain. Make sure you are in the right, about where you are hiking with your dog and try to keep the impact to a minimum by:

- Not leaving dog scat on the trail. Use plastic bags to take it to the nearest waste disposal can or bury it, if you have no bag, by the side of the trail.
- Stay on trails
- Control barking, the outdoors should be serene for everyone to enjoy.
- Keep an eye out and yield to other hikers and horses to pass.
- Do not let your dog chase wildlife.
- Take everything out that you bring in.

Trail Hazards,

This guide will describe trail surface and other specific conditions if they are important for each specific hike. However, there can always be the unexpected. Watch out for broken glass that could hurt your dog's paws. Depending on the time of year, a trail can be blanketed with nasty thorns. Thistle can become entangled in your dog's coat and hard to remove. Poison Hemlock is as it says, poisonous. Don't have Pooch eat any of it.

When hiking along logging roads, always watch out for the fast approaching trucks. This is often less of a problem on weekends, but who knows?

Your dog can transfer certain things to you, such as **ticks**. They need time to embed themselves in the skin. As it is usually about four to six hours, this gives you time to inspect your dog and yourself before it is too late. The type we are concerned with on Vancouver Island is the **Western Black-legged Tick**. The red and black females and smaller black males become grey and bean-like when they feed. They are wingless and therefore crawl and you can see the legs move. Only the mouth gets embedded below the skin. The trouble with them is, that they can carry microorganism responsible for **Lyme disease**. Fortunately here on

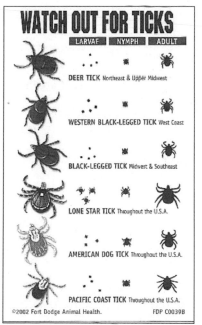

the Island, we have very few confirmed cases of the disease. Still, look for them on your pet particularly in spring and early summer. They can be found anywhere on the dog, but have a preferred area around ears, head and neck. Better still, avoid trails or hikes with tall grass and bushes. Wear long sleeves and long pants tucked into socks or boots if you plan to venture out through fields and creek-sides.

Removal of Ticks
Don't use hot cigarettes, gasoline or matches to induce the tick to detach from the skin. These are unreliable methods and can cause more harm or injury. Ticks are most safely and effectively removed by a slow and gentle pull without twisting, using tweezers or fingers. This will normally remove the tick with the mouthparts attached. The wound should be treated with an antiseptic.
For more information on ticks, visit the following web sites.
www.wyeth.com/divisions/fort_dodge.asp
www.e-ticks.net/

Wildlife encounters.
Most of the wildlife that you might encounter on Vancouver Island will not create a problem. If you expect a skunk, porcupine, raccoon or possum, keep your dog at close range. Quills from porcupines are painful to remove and your hike will change into a trip to the nearest veterinarian. Coyotes and deer are no direct danger to you or the dog, but there is the occasional Black bear and Cougar sighting. Both animals can outrun you so that is not the solution. They are usually shy and when you use a noise-making device such as a bell, they will be out of your way before you reach them. If for some reason you get surprised with a Black bear, retreat slowly and if there are cubs, never get between them and the mother. As for a cougar, the best advice is to stop and make yourself as big as possible. Take your sweater or your coat above your head and wave it around. If you need to protect your dog or yourself, use a stick or rocks in defense. This might sound simpler than it is in reality because you have to control your dog at the same time. Just keep in mind that encounters are rare and that most of the hikes in this guide are in relative urbanized areas.

Water in ponds, lakes and ocean.

Before you let your dog go for a swim or splash around, make sure that he or she is not thirsty. As ocean water is salty, drinking a large quantity is not a good idea. Standing surface water, but also fast flowing creeks and rivers are most likely infested with microscopic protozoa. They are called 'Giardia Lamblia,' a parasite that can create havoc in the intestinal system of your dog resulting in a brutal diarrhea. Therefore, always carry some fresh water for your dog and allow 'Pooch' to drink before you reach the lake or river. You can teach a dog to drink from a squirt bottle if you don't want to bring a bowl.

The weather
Here on Vancouver Island we are blessed with ideal hiking weather year round. Never too warm, humid or too cold. Still at certain times in summer, the mid-day temperature can reach uncomfortably high when you hike the Island's interior.
Dark-coated dogs absorb more sun-heat than lighter coated dogs. Realize that dogs have no sweat glands and that panting is the only way for them to disperse body heat. Therefore, dogs are more susceptible to heatstroke than humans are. Heatstroke is more likely to occur in St.Bernards, Bulldogs, and other breeds with 'pug' faces. Unusually rapid panting and a bright red tongue are signs of over-exhaustion. Get the water bottle or look for that lake or pond nearby and give "Max" a break.

Traveling on Ferries and Customs procedures with dogs

Needles to say, it is smart to be on time for ferries so that you have time to run the "doggy-walk" and "Fido's" needs are taken care of before you board the ferry. Once on the ferry, your dog is only allowed on the car-decks. Unless your dog is a guide dog, you can not take the dog to the passenger deck.

If you decide to take the dog for a walk on the car deck, keep your dog on the leash at all times and "pick up after." If you leave "Rufus" In the car, make sure there is enough ventilation and shade for the dog during the crossing, without being to inviting to strangers.

Customs requirements to bring dogs into Canada.

Fortunately for our neighbors south of the 49th parallel, the requirements are very simple. The dog owner should carry a valid certificate of the dog's Rabies vaccination. This is required for any dog older than three months. For more information, go to the following web site.
www.inspection.gc.ca/english/anima/heasan/import/dogse.shtml

A Dog's Acceptance

Say something idiotic
And nobody but a dog politely wags his tail.

Virginia Graham

Car travel with your Dog

Unfortunately, most of the 50 Best Dog Hikes are not around the corner from our home or at the end of the street. Therefore, for the more interesting hikes we have to take Jazz in the car. This used to be a love/hate situation. When her boss leaves the house, it doesn't matter where we go as long as she can come along. Most of the time she enjoys the ride, but if it is a long winding road, most likely she gets carsick pretty soon. Over the years, she must have gotten used to it, because nowadays she does much better.

Fortunately for most owners, dog traveling is much easier than in our case. However, some protective measures are prudent. Things like cages or crates can work both, protecting your car's interior as well as keeping your hands free for the driving.

If you don't like the cage idea, there are seatbelts available for dogs at specialty pet-stores. Depending on size, they range between 19 and 29 dollars.

Not all dogs enjoy the travel part, but if we prepare well, the payoff can be substantial- a happy dog, whose senses are enriched by discovering new sniffs and different surroundings.

Some helpful preparations for the trip

- To keep your dog comfortable, bring a bowl and bottled water.
- If you have a crate, use it and put some bedding in it and a favorite toy.
- Keep the dog in a contained area of the car or use seatbelts for safety.
  It looks nice, a dog roaming free in the back of a pickup truck, but what happens if you suddenly have to use the brakes? Please don't do it.
- If your dog is prone to carsickness, reduce the feeding before the trip and reduce your speed, particularly in turns.
- Bring cleaning supplies, like paper towels, poop-and-scoop bags.

Reduce the risk of loosing your pet while hiking or traveling.

Make sure you never leave without a collar secured nametag that indicates your address and phone number. For direct identification and asking around to people when your dog got away, have a colour picture with you.

A good insurance for getting your dog back is available with Vagabond Pets (see advertisement next page).

12

Who Is Getting Exercised

While it is imperative for your dog's good health to be exercised on a regular basis, we, as dog owners will also benefit from a sturdy regimen. Veterinarians quote in general that about 25 to 40 percent of dogs are obese and while it might have something to do with the food; most of it is due to lack of enough exercise.

Typically, dogs that are most prone to being overweight are often the type that are very suitable to hiking or running. These prone types are Labradors, Retrievers, Dachshunds, Beagles, Cairn Terriers, Cocker Spaniels, Collies, Shetland Sheepdogs and Basset Hounds; they will benefit most from the exercise from hiking.

Therefore, let's look at what the effects are and keep in mind what is good for your dog is even better for us. Exercise from hiking has many benefits. It not only reduces weight by burning calories but it also:

- Strengthens respiratory and circulatory systems

- Helps to get oxygen into tissue cells

- Keeps muscles toned and joints flexible

- Releases energy, relieves boredom, and keeps the mind active

- Aids in digestion

University studies have revealed that the health of dog owners is generally better than that of non-dog owners. Differences are lower blood pressure, triglyceride and cholesterol levels, which might relate to the reduced rate of heart attacks and general need of medical care.

Don't get your hopes up, but I believe that hiking dog owners should qualify for reduced life insurance rates, just as non-smokers do. Until that happens, let's seize the benefits and have our personal canine trainer take us out frequently.

Their youthful years have slipped away,
the old man and his dog.
They have a special bonding
that needs no dialogue.

From **Old Friends,** by C. David Hay

Beach Behavior

A long beach hike or just some running and splashing in and out of the water can be some of the most enjoyable moments for dogs and owners alike. However, not everyone is of the same opinion and if a young family is just having a picnic at the beach, they won't be impressed by having your dog bouncing in on their lunch or shaking off nearby.

If we want to keep those wonderful beaches accessible, we should be responsible and keep the dogs under control at all times. Obey the off-limit signs and clean-up after our pets.

On most beaches, there are scoop-bags dispensed, but on busy weekends, they might run out, so it shows better responsibility to bring some bags all the time. Waste cans are always somewhere near our accessible beaches, therefore you don't have to carry it for long.

A bit more common sense
- Don't have your dog overdo the swimming, even in good
  shape; swimming requires different sets of muscles
- try to stay close in case of problems
- Be careful in strong tides
- Don't have your dog drink salty ocean water.
  It isn't good for them even when thirsty.
- Make sure you find some shade, dogs can sunburn too,
  especially around ears and nose
- Running on soft sand is very strenuous not only for us,
  so be considerate and avoid pulling ligaments etc.

Have a great time at the beach and rinse off while you can.

Allow the experience of fresh air and the wind in my face to be pure ecstasy
Thrive on attention, and let people touch you
Avoid biting when a simple growl will do
On hot days, drink lots of water and lie under a shady tree
Delight in the simple joy of a long walk

From **What I Learned from My Dog,** *Author unknown*

Keeping the Parks Dog-Friendly

You probably hate rules and restrictions just as much as I do. I came to this country some decades ago for several reasons. One of them was the restrictions and tight regulations that were common in my home country. These things happen, need to happen when places get overcrowded and people become ignorant.

On Vancouver Island and in the Greater Victoria area specifically, we are very lucky with the park regulations and restrictions that are in place. Unlike the Greater Vancouver area, where the main rule is; dogs always leashed unless indicated differently, we can often hike the dog free in most areas unless indicated not to.
Now this is a privilege, as I feel it, that most dog owners would like to maintain. This of course is only possible if we obey the rules and reduce the impact on the park.

I live in the East Saanich community of Ten Mile Point and the shorter dogwalks are usually in that area. It is not a park, but heads off to Saanich Parks management nevertheless. It took my wife only two phone calls to have a waste-can installed at the end of a very popular chip-trail. A lot of doggy-bags are collected there and the can gets emptied on a regular basis. Everybody is happy.

The CRD regulates our Regional Parks, they recommend you keep your dogs on leash in all high use areas and watch for signs on trails and in parks where specific dog regulations apply.

Reduce Impact

Not because people are watching you, but in general, if we like to keep the parks open to our K9s, we better show good behavior at all times.
That means dogs leashed when signs indicate that.
Only hike where dogs are allowed and keep your pet on the trails.

Municipal by-laws require us to clean-up after our dogs. This is a very reasonable law and should be observed. In most parks, there are scoop-bags dispensed, but on busy weekends, they might run out, so it shows better responsibility to bring some bags all the time. Waste cans are always somewhere near. In the parks, you'll find them often by the parking lot and by other facilities.

Do not allow your dog to chase wildlife. It is an offence under CRD Parks bylaws and the BC Wildlife Act.
Avoid barking.
Don't take flowers or anything else.
Leave only footprints behind, take everything out that you take in.

Enjoy your walks and hikes

Welcome to our trail walks.
This is a great opportunity to get together and socialize with each other and our dogs

HERE'S HOW:

√ Pick up your dog's poop and your own litter.

√ Keep your dog on a leash walking to and from your vehicle.

√ Leaving dogs unattended is prohibited.

√ Dogs' licence and vaccinations must be current.
√ Carry dog treats at your own risk.

√ Do not bring people food with you.

√ Be aware of your dog and closely supervise at all times.

√ Leave the area cleaner than when you came.

AND LET'S REMEMBER:

√ We are responsible for our dog's behaviour.

√ Each one of us is legally and financially liable for our own dog's behaviour.

√ Dogs will chase a running child or person.

√ Unvaccinated dogs, especially puppies, are vulnerable to disease and parasites.

THE FOLLOWING ARE NOT PERMITTED

√ Female dogs in heat
√ Dogs that are injured or ill
√ Puppies under 11 weeks of age
√ Aggressive dogs which are not muzzled and not in training for their behaviour problems.

It's the Bark Hour

Through our walks, we're promoting a gathering of dogs and their companions for a social time of exercise and fun for all.

We would appreciate any feedback on problems or suggestions on how we can improve the walks and the experience.

For inquiries or concerns please contact Peni at www.islanddogsports.com

18

Locater Map, Victoria and Saanich Peninsula

Swartz Bay
Sidney
P8
P7
P5
P9
P10
Hwy # 17
P6
P4
P1
P2
P3
P11
V11 V10
V9
Trans
V8 V5
V12 V6 V7
Canada Hwy # 1 V4
V1 V3
Victoria
N
V2

10 km

19

V 1 Beacon Hill Park, Victoria

Trail difficulty 🐾
Trail condition ☺
Time/length 3km around
Admission None
Parking Free
Hours dawn to dusk
Restrictions North of Dallas Rd dogs should be leashed at all times
Overall Rating 🦴🦴🦴

Park information

Located at the foot of Douglas Street, a delightful quiet envelops this sunny spot in Victoria. There is a variety of open spaces with natural habitat, winding paths along ponds and lakes and beautiful landscaped park areas. A wonderful mixture of exotic and native trees, including Garry Oak, Arbutus, Douglas fir, Western Red Cedar, birch, willow and maples grow throughout the park. In the center, you can find an alpine- and rock garden.

Walking trails link with neighbouhood streets that lead into the busy hum

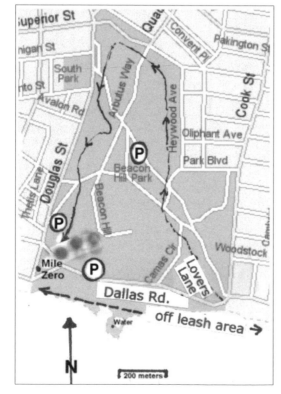

of commercial activity. From the south end, the open space surrounding the world's tallest freestanding totem pole has several unofficial trails. One called **Camas Circle** is a nice one to take, so is **Lovers Lane**, particularly a good choice if you parked near the southeast corner of the park.

Walking north along **Heywood Way**, one reaches the playground, public washrooms and further north-west, the Beacon Hill Children's Farm. Return along **Bridge Way**, and you will see the ponds and lake. The complete perimeter of the park is about three kilometers. However, following the winding paths, one can easily make a one hour stroll. **Note:** The best free

20

roaming dog-playground is just across **Dallas Road**. Wide grassy spaces, ocean access and spectacular views offer a combination that makes that section of the park 🦴🦴🦴🦴🦴 **rating**.

A bit of history
Beacon Hill Park is the grand showpiece of Victoria, a city with a long and proud tradition of gardening. Set aside in 1858 by James Douglas, Governor of Vancouver Island, the 75-hectare (200 acre) plot of land was officially established as a park in 1882. Beacon Hill was named after a pair of masts strategically placed on a hill to act as a range-beacon, a navigational aid to mariners approaching Victoria's inner harbour.
Before the settlers, this area was traditional Salish Indian territory. One unique attraction that still stands today is the 38.8-meter (128-foot) pole, which was once the world's tallest totem. It was created by Mungo Martin, not a Salish but a Kwakwaka'wakw artist in 1956. In 2002, it was restored to its original splendour.

Trail sense
Keep the dog on a leash and clean-up after. There are usually people around with children and the waterfowl in the lakes could be disturbed easily, even by a good-natured retriever.

Bonus
Listen for Herons in the tops of Douglas fir and keep your eyes open for a home-pair of Bald Eagles that live nearby. There are facilities at several points in the park and just across from the biggest off leash playground in town.

Swimming
Not available in this section of the park, but right adjacent, across **Dallas Road** is the ocean front part of the park where dogs are free to roam and perhaps go for a dip in the ocean. (See **Clover Point to Ogden Point** hike)

Directions to get there
Beacon Hill Park is located at **Mile Zero** of the Trans Canada Highway, the southern most point of Victoria's downtown..
Follow Douglas Street all the way south and park the car according to the parking signs. At the south end, there is plenty of parking on Dallas Rd. Most spots have 1.5 to 3.5 hrs. maximum, plenty of time to enjoy the park. You will also find a free parking lot on the circular drive near the Children's Farm.
🚗 About five minutes from downtown Victoria.

V 2   Dallas Rd. Clover to Ogden Point, Victoria

Trail difficulty   🐾
Trail condition   ☺
Time/ length 3 km one-way
Admission   None
Parking Free to 50 c/2Hrs
Hours Open year round
Restrictions Outside the large 'Off Leash' area, dogs should be leashed and everywhere owners should clean-up after Pooch.
Overall Rating 🦴🦴🦴🦴🦴

Park information
One of the best hikes/ walks in Victoria, not only because it has a huge off leash section for your dog with beach access, but also for the spectacular views of the Olympic Mountains, the Strait of Juan de Fuca, and the never ending sounds of the splashing waves that you follow all the way.

Clover Point is at the east end of this hike. It has an access road and free parking while your dog is right in 'Dog heaven'. From here to **Mile 0 at Douglas Street**, about two kilometers further, this is the largest off-leash playground in Victoria.

A good hike follows the winding path into **Beacon Hill Park**, part of the ocean front chain of open parkland. You pass **Finlayson Point** that has a shelter if one is needed. By Douglas Street, you reach the sidewalk and Pooch should be leashed on if you follow the sidewalk to **Ogden Point**. However, there is an alternative that could be more fun. Across from the second side street, Paddon Street, is **Fonyo Beach** where at low tide you could continue below the sidewalk and reach **Holland Point Park**. You can also follow the sidewalk a bit further and follow the hike through Holland Point Park along the cliffside ocean. At the end of this park, you reach the sidewalk again for the last half kilometer before reaching **Ogden Point** (5-6 km return)

One can start this hike also at **Ogden Point** where parking meters charge only 50 c. for two hours. Dogs are not allowed on the breakwater, but there is a path below on the inside that shows you all the hustle and bustle that goes on when cruise ships are in town.

A bit of history
As with so many names in and around Victoria, they relate either to the early explorers or to the Hudson Bay Company. In 1843, Ogden Point was named after Peter Skene Ogden, a Hudson Bay Company man. The 800-meter breakwater was built much later and lays along an underwater trail used much by divers nowadays.

Sir James Douglas, Governor, landed at Clover Point when he came the first time with the Beaver in 1843, and called the point after the purple-reddish flowers that must have been in full bloom at the time of his arrival.

Trail sense
Pick up after your dog. Plenty of waste cans are scattered around this area, so you don't have to carry it for long.

Swimming
Yes, there is swimming for Pooch at the beaches between Douglas Street and Clover Point to the east. Watch out on rough days, the waves and current might be too much for Pooch.
Opposite San Jose Ave. just left of Oswego, is another beach access point by steps.

Bonus
A special doggie water fountain is in the center of the **Beacon Hill Park** ocean front section. Watch for colourful kites at **Clover** and **Finlayson Points**. The big ones are surf-gliders. They will only stop after the wind dies, always trying to get more air and higher speed. The same counts for the surfers that use the same area.
Check out the Mile 0 monument across Douglas Street and the once-largest totem pole in the world that is further into **Douglas Park** (see there). There are public washrooms at the corner of Cook Street and Dallas Road, opposite the nice B & B.

Directions to get there Follow the Trans-Canada Highway south. It is called Douglas Street in Victoria, and follow it to Mile 0. Here it hits a T junction at Dallas Rd. Here you will find free parking on the ocean side all along the road when you turn left. You can go on to Clover Point, less than 2 km and park there.

🚗 Five minutes from downtown.

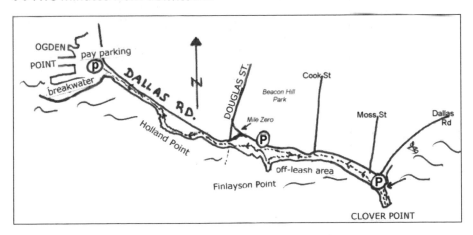

23

V 3   Willows Beach, Oak Bay

Trail difficulty   🐾
Condition   ☺
Walking Time < 1 hr
Admission   None
Parking   Free
Hours dawn to dusk
Restrictions No dogs on beach from May 1 to Sept. 30
Overall Rating 🦴🦴🦴🦴

Beach information

This is a nice sandy beach of about one kilometer long with an easterly exposure and fantastic scenery. On a clear day, you might see the Olympic Mountains, Mt. Baker and even Mt. Rainier beyond Seattle.
Facilities, a water-fountain and concession make this an excellent destination most of the year.

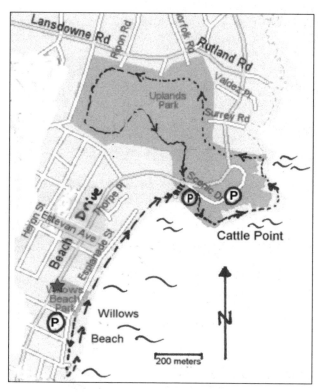

Swimming

Some of the best ocean swimming within the city limmits. However, even with the sun warming the shallow water at the beach all day, it still is pretty chilly most of the time. Your dog wouldn't mind it, and that's what counts, so go for it.

Bonus

From Willows Beach, you can extend the walk if you like. At the end of Esplanade, hike up along the steps to **Cattle Point and Uplands Park** (see there). It offers even better panoramic views, but has no sandy beach.

24

Directions to get there

From downtown Victoria, follow Fort Street all the way to where is turns into Cadboro Bay Road. After the road makes a clear turn north, you will soon see Estevan Street where you turn right. You will see the ocean come up in front. Cross Beach Drive and find parking on Esplanade or drive a bit south on Beach Drive and find a spot at **Willows Park** on Dalhousie Street.

🚗 Allow about 15 minutes from downtown.

V 4　Cattle Point and Uplands Park, Oak Bay

Trail difficulty　🐾

Trail condition　☺

Time/ length < 1 hr

Admission　None

Parking　Free

Hours dawn to dusk

Restrictions On leash during April May and June

Overall Rating 🦴🦴🦴🦴

Park information

A nice 75 acres of diverse park that is divided by Beach Drive. This road cuts the park into a beautiful but rather small ocean side **Cattle Point,** and the larger **Uplands Park** walking area. The latter offers plenty of winding, comfortable trails among the gnarly Garry Oaks and other woodland. **See map previous page, with Willows Beach.**

Despite its urban setting, Cattle Point offers some of the best tide pools near the city among rugged rocky outcrops. It is also a great spot to watch sailing races held regularly on weekends and seals and other wildlife in the nearby kelp-beds.

If you like to take Pooch for a good game of throw and catch, Cattle Point offers a great play area with fantastic scenery. On a clear day, you might see the Olympic Mountains, Mt. Baker and even Mt. Rainier beyond Seattle.

A bit of history

History has it that besides cattle that were forced to swim to this shore from delivery ships anchored out in the bay, this same point was a busy departure spot for a lot of bootlegging during the prohibition.

Trail sense

The rocky outcrops are very rough and slippery, so watch your step at Cattle Point. The leash restriction is during nesting season, so for a good reason. Please obey it.

Swimming

There are good spots for an eager dog to hit the salty ocean.

See map previous page, with Willows Beach.

Bonus

From Cattle Point, one can extend a hike down at the south end along a set of steps to **Esplanade** and **Willows Beach** (see there). It offers the same panoramic views, but there is a nice sandy beach all the way. Watch for the signs that indicate a seasonal leash restriction at **Willows Beach**. Facilities with water and a consession make this an excellent stopover.

Directions to get there

From downtown Victoria, follow Fort Street up all the way to where it turns into Cadboro Bay Road. After the road makes a clear turn north, you will soon see Estevan Street, where you turn right. The ocean is coming up in front, but take a left on Beach Drive. Where it turns to the right, you will see the one-way entrance to Cattle Point parking and boat ramps coming up on the right. You'll find a good trail chart at the larger, oceanfront parking area.

🚗 Allow about 15 minutes from downtown.

V 5   Cadboro Bay Beach, Gyro Park, East Saanich

Access difficulty 🐾 - 🐾🐾
Condition ☺
Walking Time < 1 hr
Admission None
Parking Free
Hours dawn to dusk
Restrictions No dogs in specified beach area after 9 am from May to August.
Overall Rating 🦴🦴🦴🦴

Beach information

This is a very nice crested sandy beach. More than one-kilometer in length, it has an ideal southern exposure. Fantastic views of the Olympic Mountains in Washington State can be enjoyed on most days. If the wind from the ocean is too strong, there is a large grassy area to run your dog. You will find it behind the playground to the east. It gives some protection from the predominantly southeasterly winds.

On a low tide, the beach can be several hundred feet wide as the sandy bottom lowers very gradually into Cadboro Bay. This shallow aspect makes it a very safe beach and improves the water temperature.

Good facilities and a water-fountain make this an excellent in town destination year round. Large amounts of driftwood can sometimes make the beach access a bit difficult.

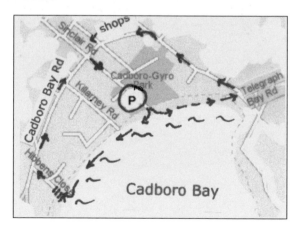

Circular walk

There are two options here. Take a beach walk to either side and it will lead you to a steep set of stairs at **Hibbens Close** when you go west. Going east leads to only a few steps at the foot of **Telegraph Bay Road**. This section is open for dogs all year. This is Naz Rayani's favorite walk. When he takes a short break from his busy Pharmacy, he usually takes the beach to the right and tackles the steep flight of stairs at **Hibbens Close**. Both sides bring you back on Cadboro Bay Road. Walk back to the pleasant little shopping village where you can pick up anything from

latte's and sandwiches at Olive Olio's Pasta & Espresso Bar, newspapers, magazines or books next door, to quality pet products at Chez Terry's.
If you'd rather avoid the steep stairs up, take the walk the other way around. Go from the parking lot back to **Cadboro Bay Road**. Take a left until **Hibbens Close** and take the steps down to follow the beach left.

Swimming
Some of the best ocean swimming within the city limits. The water is usually warmer than at **Willows Beach** (see there), but that also means more algae, which is less than pleasant at times. Your dog won't mind it, so have a blast.

Directions to get there
From downtown Victoria, follow Fort Street all the way to where it turns into Cadboro Bay Road. Follow this road all the way past the Uplands Golf Course (on your left) down to the little shopping village where you take a right on Sinclair Road to a large parking lot.
🚗 Allow about 15 minutes from downtown.

V 6   Cedar Hill Park, East Saanich

Trail difficulty   🐾
Trail condition   ☺
Time/ length 1 hour around
Admission   None
Parking   Free
Hours dawn to dusk
Restrictions Dogs should be leashed near the ponds.
Overall Rating 🦴🦴🦴

Park information

A 3.5 km (2.2 miles) picturesque jogging/nature trail surround the Cedar Hill Golf course and is accessible from several points around the park. At the north end is the delightful **Kings Pond**, with many ducks and birds around. A bird Identification sign helps you to see which kinds are usually around.

The park is like an oasis, large open fields sloping slowly downward from North to South. While the park is surrounded by friendly neighbourhoods, it feels far removed from the city's hustle and bustle. Secluded areas suddenly give way to majestic views over contorted Garry Oak, past **Barwick Lake** and beyond the city of Victoria. On a clear day one can see the magical blue reflection of the ocean and the Olympic Mountains beyond. The trail is very pleasantly padded with soft cedar chips in large areas on the Northeast side. You'll find some hardtop towards the south, and elsewhere, well-maintained gravel. The entire trail is a good hour's workout. You can shorten the trail midway, crossing the links by the clubhouse and parking lot.

A bit of history

The park is situated in the middle of town, and although this course has been in operation since the 1930's, the course was known as the "Cow Pasture" for a reason. The Corporation of Saanich purchased it in 1969 and it currently operates as a volunteer organization. It has the reputation as "The Friendliest Golf Club" around, and has steadily developed into one of the most popular courses in Canada.

Trail sense

Particularly around the **Kings Pond** at the north-end, dogs should be on the leash. A number of joggers use the trails at times, and if your dog is o.k. with that, Pooch can enjoy more freedom in this park. Since the walk is around a golf course, for your safety, stay on the well-marked trail.

Bonus

There is a clubhouse with facilities and restaurant in the center of the park. Both are open to the public. The clubhouse combines sensational views of the area with fantastic food and has a fully licensed lounge named "Shank's Pub." Usually there is a pail of water outside for Pooch.

30

Swimming
While there is the lake and pond, swimming is not permitted, even for friendly dogs.

Directions to get there
From downtown, take Douglas Street north to Hillside, where you turn right. Take a left on Cook Street and follow this only briefly to Finlayson where you turn right. Almost immediately you will see a parking lot on the left where you can park between 6 am and 11 pm.
🚗 About 10 minutes from downtown Victoria.

From the north into town, take McKenzie to the left untill Cedar Hill Cross Road, which you take to the right. Just past Blenkinsop, take Ascoth to the end and you see a small parking lot at Kings Pond.

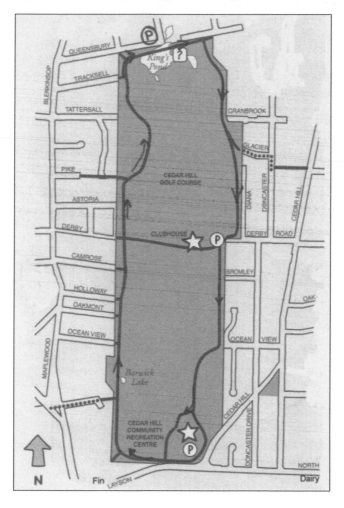

V 7   Mount Tolmie Park, East Saanich

Trail difficulty   🐾 🐾
Trail condition   ☺
Time/ length <1 hour around
Admission   None
Parking   Free
Hours   6 am – 11 pm
Restrictions   None, but dogs on-leash is recommended
Overall Rating 🦴🦴🦴

Park information

This is a small park in an urban setting, but with the climb of almost 400 feet, it can make a great workout for both, you and the dog. Named after the biologist Dr. William Frazer Tolmie, the trails in this park run up first on the east side of the road and later on both sides. Staying east of Mayfair to the summit is less steep than crossing the road. **Bring binoculars** for the wonderful panoramic views over the Greater Victoria area. On clear days, the Olympic Mountain Range and Mount Baker in the Cascades are breathtaking.

The large flat concrete structure near the summit is a water reservoir to bring up the pressure in the kitchen and bathroom taps.

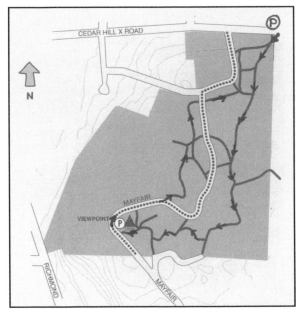

Trail sense

On weekends, it can be busy on top. Keep your dog under control at all time and stay on the paths as to preserve the many varieties of native wildflowers.

Bonus

Besides a great view from the top, there are picnic tables along the way.

Directions to get there

From downtown, take Douglas Street north to Hillside, where you turn right. Take a left on Shelbourne Street and follow this to Cedar Hill X Road. Here at the lights, take a right, go past Richmond and the park will show up on your right. Park at Gordon Head Road or Cedar Hill X Road, past the light. The trail starts right at the intersection.

You can also turn right at Mayfair and drive to the top where there is plenty of parking as well. 🚗 Allow 15 minutes from downtown.

Lochside Regional Trail, South part East Saanich   # V 8

Trail difficulty 🐾
Trail condition ☺
Time/ length <1 hour
Admission None
Parking Free
Hours Dawn to Dusk
Restrictions Dogs must be leashed at all times
Overall Rating 🦴🦴

Trail information
This is an urban section of the Lochside Trail that branches off at the highway overpass from the **Galloping Goose Trail** (see there). As well as the "Goose," this trail makes use of the old Canadian National Railway bed and is therefore quite straight and level.

Walk North of the city
From the highway overpass to Quadra Street is a short distance of under two kilometers, but this is a wonderful urban and pastoral section worthwhile when you need a short walk. The city noise disappears once you go through the ravine, and once out from there, the pristine setting of Swan Lake makes this section even more attractive (stay on trail, dogs are not allowed in park). A nice wide trestle followed by a green section make this walk about 3.5 km for a return trip if one turns around at Quadra Street.

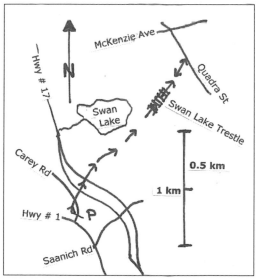

Trail sense
Since you have to share this trail with cyclists, joggers and in-line skaters, stay to the right and pick up after your dog.

Swimming None

Directions to get there
From downtown Victoria, follow Douglas Street north past Mayfair Mall. Take a right at the lights on Saanich Road and go to the left to turn into the parking area of Town and Country Shopping Center. Park somewhere at the far back.
Walk across Carey Road and you will see the acces point for the trail.
🚗 About 10 minutes from downtown.

V 9 Lochside Regional Trail, North part East Saanich

Trail difficulty 🐾
Trail condition ☺
Time/ length 1-2 hrs
Admission None
Parking Free
Hours Dawn to Dusk
Restrictions Dogs must be leashed at all times
Overall Rating 🦴🦴🦴

Trail information
This is an easy, level trail through woods, and pastoral landscape you would not expect so close to urbanization. Shortly after the start, there is a nice long trestle taking you over **Blenkinsop Lake** where you could spot rare and uncommon bird-species.

The trail makes use of the old Canadian National Railway bed and is therefore quite straight and definitely level. Up until Royal Oak Road, the trail is about 3.5 km, so a return hike could take more than an hour and a half.

You can make this hike even longer by crossing Royal Oak Ave onto Lochside Drive. Soon you will see the foot and bike path leaving the road. Another 3 kilometers bring you to the Cordova Bay Golf course and Adrienne's Tea Garden at Mattick's Farm where the lovely gift-shop **A Stable Way of Life** has an eclectic collection of specialty giftware for animal lovers of all kind.

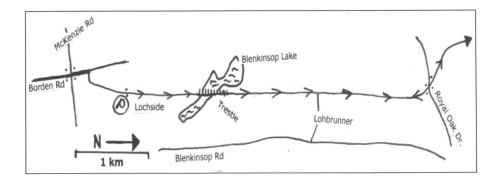

Trail sense
Since you have to share this trail with cyclists and possibly horses, stay to the right and pick up after your dog.

Swimming None

Directions to get there

From downtown Victoria, take Blanshard Street north to the McKenzie exit where you take a right. After about 1.5 km, just after the busy Quadra Street intersection take a left on Borden Street. Behind the Motor License Office is Lochside where you'll find good parking at the end, past Munn Excavating.

It's about 6 km, so allow yourself about 15 - 20 minutes.

From the west, into town by Highway # 1, turn left at McKenzie and follow the instructions above.

From the Swartz Bay Ferry, Highway # 17 south you could easy start at Matticks Farm. Take the Cordova Bay Rd. exit and soon you will find parking on your left near the shops at Matticks Farm. Less than 20 minutes from the ferry.

35

V 10   Thetis Lake Regional Park, Victoria

Trail difficulty 🐾🐾 - 🐾🐾🐾

Trail condition ☺ - ☹

Time/ length 5 km +

Admission   Free

Parking $ 2.00 per day from May 1 – Sept. 30

Hours 8 a.m. to sunset

Restrictions Dogs must be leashed when passing through main picnic or beach areas and are not allowed to stay between June 1 and Sept. 15. Many changes are proposed. On leash and off leash sections/times and possible more designated splash areas. Watch for the latest info posted at the kiosk.

Overall Rating 🦴🦴🦴🦴🦴 (as long as off-leash persist)

Park information

This huge, 778 hectares park is a very popular 'nice weather' destination since the lakes warm up quickly and are fresh-water. However, if you pass the two beach areas where most of the visitors settle for, you'll find a relatively quiet park that offers miles of hikes with a good variety in difficulty.

Spring is very colourful in this park with a great abundance of wild flowers. Douglas fir offers some shaded parts for your hike. Hiking trails over rocky outcrops covered in moss can be slippery at times but the views through Arbutus and Garry Oak are stunning.

A bit of history

Thetis Lake's name is after a Royal Navy 36 gun frigate H.M.S. Thetis that was stationed in Esquimalt in the mid eighteen hundreds. It had a patrol function during the gold rush and was responsible for the area from Victoria to the Queen Charlotte Islands.

In 1885, the lake changed from private hands to the Esquimalt Waterworks Company and supplied Victoria and Esquimalt. The trails were put in around the 1930 to keep unemployed workers busy. In 1932, the lake was officially open for the public. Where once a tearoom and a dance pavilion were is now a concession. In 1993, the CRD acquired the park from the City of Victoria.

Hikes

From the parking lot, take the short paved road into the park. At the entrance, there is a clear marking system setup and the easiest but still very pretty hike is the **Lower Thetis Lake Trail**. One can keep the hike short by turning south at the head of the lower lake and take **Trillium Trail** back to the second beach and parking lot. This would take less than an hour.

A longer option, about twice the time, is to circumnavigate both lakes. At the head of the lower lake, one continues on the **Upper Thetis Lake Trail**, which is quite a bit longer.

Seymour Hill (if not yet off limits for dogs)

For a good workout, and rewarding views take the **Seymour Hill Trail** from the map kiosk at the parking lot. You will see it on the right. It takes you up through Douglas fir forest and later into more open Garry Oak and Arbutus woodland. Keep left to avoid the ecological sensitive **Lewis Clark Trail** (restriction proposed at time of writing). While going up and down, you get some nice views before you reach the top.

The 131-meter summit has a directional cairn with sight lines to the local mountains. It is a great picnic spot with awesome views over the nearby lakes.

You can make this a circular hike if you like. Find the trail down at the other side. It is on the left when your back is turned to the lakes. Watch out for the first portion. It is steep. Keeping left will get you down to the lake and the last part will follow the **Lower Thetis Lake Trail** back to the parking lot. This circle would take you 1 to 1.5 hours. You can make it even longer by turning right at **Lower Thetis Lake Trail** and follow the trails described above.

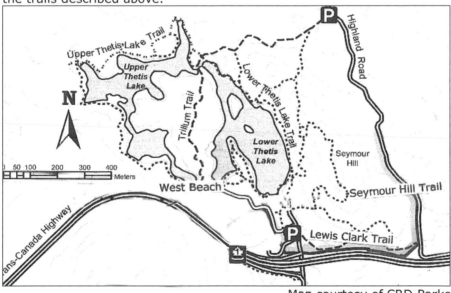

Map courtesy of CRD Parks

Trail sense

In summer, the moss on the bedrock gets very dry and cigarette butt or a match could spark a disaster. Please be careful and avoid fire.

Swimming

Go to **West Beach**, it has no restrictions for dogs, or try further along the **Lower Lake Trail**, past the main beach.

Directions to get there

Follow the Trans-Canada Highway from Victoria, and take the Colwood exit. Follow the Old Island Highway. Turn right on Six Mile Road, which leads to the park by going underneath the highway.

V 11   Goldstream, Provincial Park, Langford

Trail difficulty 🐾 - 🐾🐾🐾
Trail condition ☺ ☺
Time/ length 2– 3 hrs
Admission   None
Parking $ 1.00 - $ 3.00
Hours sunrise to sunset
Restrictions Keep dogs leashed at all times
Overall Rating 🦴🦴🦴🦴

Park information
This is a park with a tremendous diversity of flora and fauna, making it a
unique and popular destination. You can tell how much mist and rain
develops here from the many mosses and lichens flourishing here. The
lower section of the park has its own eco-zone with 600-year-old
Douglas fir and western red cedar while higher up, stands of Garry oak
and arbutus, found exclusively on Vancouver Island and the southwest
coast of BC, have their own dryer zone. In fall and early winter, the
Goldstream River is the site of a spectacular annual Chum, Coho and
Chinook salmon spawning run. During this time, eagle spotting is as easy
as car spotting on a highway. The eagles have come back in large
numbers and during low tide, you can follow their eating habits best.
Other wildlife is abundant here as well. The park is host to black bears,
cougars and deer, as well as numerous small animals like raccoons,
minks, beavers, otters and squirrels.

A bit of History
Goldstream Park is located on traditional fishing grounds of the local First
Nations. Mining shafts and tunnels from way back are all that remain of
the gold rush that this area experienced during the mid-19th century.
The Greater Victoria Water Board donated the park to the people of
British Columbia in 1958.

Hikes
An extensive network of trails winds itself through this park, totaling a
distance of approximately 16 km. You will find a steep, rugged, difficult
one to **Mount Finlayson**. Follow the Finlayson Arm Road and after about
200 meters, take the trail up on the right. The huge elevation to cover
before you reach the 419-meter summit will stretch your time anywhere
from over one to two hours and up, depending on you and your dog's
stamina. This is not an easy hike, so be prepared.
The one we did is long, circular, but has options for escape midway.
Start from the parking lot and take the **Visitor Center Trail** north.
Follow the Niagara Creek if the water level allows this, through the
tunnel underneath the highway. If that is impossible, you have to cross
the busy highway, so be careful and pick up the trail to the **Niagara
Falls**. They are quite spectacular in the rainy season, and make sure you

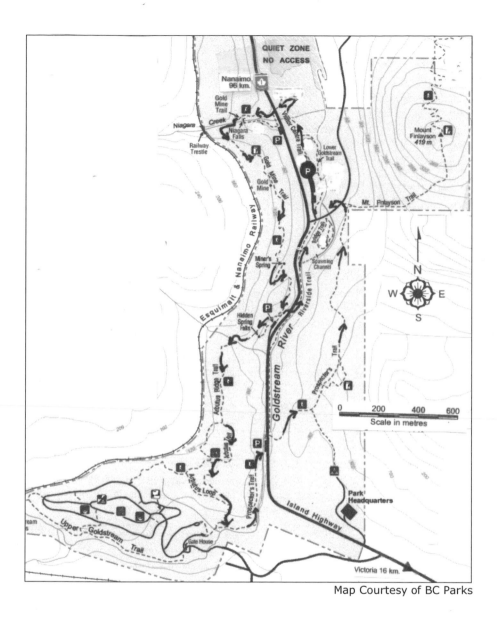

Map Courtesy of BC Parks

get there via the trail on the north side. Past the waterfall, you can cross to the south side of the creek, and pick up the **Gold Mine Trail** for a few kilometers. You will hear the traffic when you get close to the highway again. Here is your midway escape if you'd like to shorten the hike. (Cross the road again and pick up the **Riverside Trail** north, back to the parking area, 1.5 – 2 hours total) If you decide to continue, follow the **Arbutus Ridge Trail**, keep left until you reach, at the south end the **Prospector's Trail** and follow this north. By a parking area, cross the highway and keep on Prospector's Trail all the way back to Finlayson Arm Road where you take a short left to get to the parking area on the right. Total length of this hike is 2 to 3 hours depending on your speed.

Trail sense
During the sensitive salmon spawning time, dogs must be kept out of the river. They should be leashed at all time. The ecosystems of this park are rare and fragile. Shortcutting trails destroy plant life and soil structure, so please don't.

Swimming There is no designated swimming area at this park; however, there are some sections of the Goldstream River near the campground that may be used for swimming.

Directions to get there
Take Douglas Street and follow the Trans-Canada Highway from Victoria past Millstream and Langford. Watch for the Park Headquarters coming up on the right and shortly after, the parking area will be on the same side.
 Approximately 30 minutes from Victoria.

Galloping Goose Regional Trail, Victoria Section, # V 12

Trail difficulty 🐾
Trail condition ☺
Time/ length 1 hr +
Admission None
Parking Free
Hours Dawn to Dusk
Restrictions Dogs must be under control
Overall Rating 🦴🦴

Trail information

This picturesque multi-use trail has a large variety of landscapes and is always easy to walk. It was formerly a railway line. The trail runs through urban, rural and wilderness scenery for 55 kilometres from Victoria to Sooke. The Galloping Goose Regional Trail, established in 1987, was named for the gas-powered passenger car that carried mail and up to 30 passengers twice daily between Victoria and Sooke during the 1920s. It is part of the **Trans-Canada Trail**, a national multi-use trail system linking trails from coast to coast. "The Goose" intersects with the **Lochside Trail,** a 29-kilometre former railway line that runs from Saanich to Sidney.

Hiking sections recommended

Here I will discus an in-town section that is easily accessible and gives you the feel of being out of the city. There are other sections, truly out of town. Look for **Matheson Lake** and **Roche Cove** Regional Parks in this guide.

In the City

From the Point Ellice Bridge to the highway overpass is 2.5 km. It is an urban section however, with marvelous views from the lengthy trestle bridge over the Selkirk Water inlet, you feel far removed from urban life. This is followed by a nice section through the Cecelia Ravine before you will go through a

41

mixed urban, but quiet area reaching the overpass. Return is the same way, unless you have made other arrangements.

Trail sense
Since you have to share this trail with cyclists, joggers and inn-line skaters, stay to the right and pick up after your dog.

Swimming None

Directions to get there
From Douglas Street, turn west on Pandora Avenue and cross the (Blue) Johnson Street bridge. Then take the seccond street on the right, Tyee Road. Go to the end and park before the lights or at the Wilson Shopping center on the left. Cross the bussy street at the lights and pickup the trail right in front.

🚗 Less than five minutes from downtown.

Elk and Beaver Lake, Regional Park, East Saanich # P 1

Trail difficulty 🐾
Trail condition ☺
Time/ length 1 – 3 hrs
Admission None
Parking Free
Hours sunrise to sunset

Restrictions From June 1 to Sept.15, dogs must be leashed and are allowed to pass through but not stay at the following areas: Beaver, Hamsterly, Eagle and Water Ski beaches and picnic areas.

Overall Rating 🦴🦴🦴🦴

Park information

The large lakes are connected and surrounded by a 10 km walking trail that leads through forest, fields and wetlands. For about one-third of the length, the trail is shared with horses or bicycles. There are shorter hikes possible, particularly on the south eastside of the lakes.

In the early 1900s, both lakes were used for water supply for Victoria. Old filter beds at the south end of Beaver Lake are now filled in and used as a large parking lot. There are many access points. Look at the directions below for two good ones.

Circular hike

Leave the parking lot and aim for dog-friendly **North Beach** on Beaver Lake. Here, take a left turn to circumnavigate the lakes in a clockwise manner. At the south end, **Beaver Beach**, follow part of the hike/bridle trail on your right, going North West. At a short distance, you can leave the bridle trail and follow the shore somewhat closer. Eventually you get back on the bridle trail, which turns into a cycling trail when you reach the west shore of Elk Lake, using most of the old bed from the Victoria to Sidney railway. Follow this all the way to the north-end, past the fishing pier and **Waterski Beach**. At the boat ramp, the trail becomes strictly hiking again. Continue on a nice level section to **Hamsterly Beach** where you turn south. Past the rowing club, you come to **Eagle Beach** where the trail can be followed still along the shore before you are back at your parking area.

Trail sense

Many deer in the area necessitate you to keep your dog at close range. When sharing the path with others, a leashed dog makes a lot of sense.

Swimming

Several beaches around the lakes are not off limits for dogs in summer. Since this is a freshwater lake, swimming can be very pleasant, which makes it worthwhile to look for the right places. **North Beach**, on the east side of Beaver Lake is easy accessible and near the parking area. **Creeds**, which is across from Ski Beach and **Wooten's Beach** near

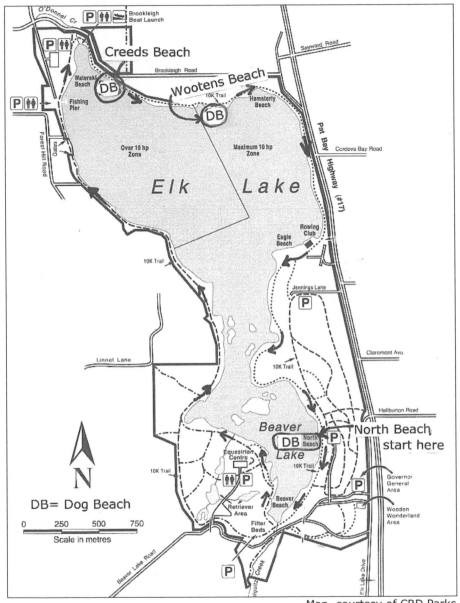

Map, courtesy of CRD Parks

Hamsterly Beach, are two options on the north shore of Elk Lake.
South of the Equestrian Center, on both sides of the entrance road, are special retriever ponds. This area is under license agreement and one should consult the local retriever club for access

Directions to get there

Beaver Lake Entrance
From downtown Victoria, take Blanshard Street north and follow the Pat Bay Highway, and take the Royal Oak Drive exit. Turn left on Royal Oak Drive to cross over the Highway, then right on Elk Lake Drive to reach the parking lot.

Elk Lake Entrance
Follow the Pat Bay Highway from Victoria. Turn left on Sayward Road (north from the Beaver Lake entrance), a short left again on Hamsterly Road, then right on Brookleigh Road, which leads to the parking lot on the left.
🚗 20 minutes from Victoria.

P 2   Lone Tree Hill, Regional Park, Highlands

Trail difficulty 🐾🐾 - 🐾🐾
Trail condition   ☺
Time/ length   2.5 km
Admission   None
Parking   Free
Hours sunrise to sunset
Restrictions Keep dogs under control
Overall Rating 🦴🦴🦴

Park information

This is a relative small park, but the hike to the summit can be challenging and rewarding particularly in spring. That is when wildflowers such as fawn lilies, shooting stars and common camas blanket the open woodlands. There used to be a bonsai-like Douglas-fir near the summit, which was designated a "Heritage Tree." It wasn't very tall, but stood there for ages by itself. Now you can find rare and beautiful plants nestled in the steep, dry rock faces.

Hike to the summit

The trail starts from the parking area on Millstream Road and climbs steadily up, first in northerly direction, then turns clockwise and zigzags southward to a very fine viewpoint. With the Malahat to the west, the Gowlland Range and Olympic Mountains in other directions, this is a great spot for bird watching. Bald eagles, red-tailed hawks and turkey vultures are common here. There is no loop hike here, so return the same way as you came.

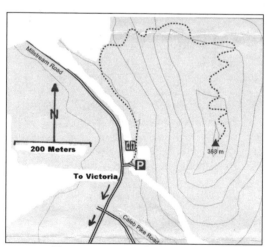
Map courtesy of CRD Parks

Trail sense

You are in the Highlands, known for a lot of wildlife. Keep your dog near and under control.

Swimming None

Directions to get there

Take Douglas Street and follow the Trans-Canada Highway from Victoria. Take the Millstream Road exit.
Turn right on Millstream Road and continue to the junction of Millstream Lake Road.

Turn left to continue on Millstream Road to the park entrance which is on the right.

🚗 Approximately 30 minutes from Victoria.

46

Francis/ King Regional Park, Victoria

Trail difficulty 🐾 - 🐾 🐾
Trail condition ☺ -☹
Time/ length 2-11 km
Admission None
Parking Free

Hours 8 a.m. – 9 p.m. April to October 8- 5 October to April
Restrictions, a proposal is underway to make this an all times 'on-leash' park.

Overall Rating 🦴🦴🦴

Park information

This is an excellent park to learn and explore nature. A great variety of terrain is offered, from rain forest and swamp, to dryer rocky ledges and woodland. When you have guests visiting from out of town, and want to impress them with some really big trees, this is your closest call to town. One can make short, 1 km trails, intermediate or long hikes that extend into **Thetis Lake Regional Park**. A Nature Centre at the parking lot is open noon to 4 pm on Saturdays, Sundays and holiday Mondays and is staffed by volunteers and CRD Parks staff.

A bit of history

Two generous people donated most of the parklands. Tommy Francis in 1960 and Freeman King, better known as Skipper who was a naturalist, did this later. The boardwalk is named for Skipper's wife, Elsie who was a prominent leader in the Victoria Girl Guides. In 1979, the park as we now know it was established.

Hikes

The shortest is the wheelchair accessible **Elsie King Trail**. At time of writing, this is the only area in the park where dogs have to be leashed.
The **Heritage Tree Walk** is a 15-minute hike that passes by giant Douglas-fir trees near the creek. Cross the road at the parking lot and go through the wooden horse gate. The trail slopes down into a forested creek bed. Before you reach that however, you walk through a huge fallen tree, like a gateway. Cross the creek and shortly after your paths cross. Take a right for a short while and by the next junction (**Centennial Trail**) keep right again. Here is the tallest, 245 feet Douglas-fir tree. When you cross the creek-bed again, you find on the left the thickest tree, 9.9 feet. Follow the trail uphill and you reach another horse gate where at the road you turn right and will soon be at the parking lot again.
A serious hike in this park is the **Centennial Trail**. You can start this trail at several points. One is from leaving the **Heritage Trail**, after you have seen the 'giants'. Another option is direct from the parking lot behind the Nature Centre. Take the **Centennial** to the right. This will take you counter clockwise around most of the park and might take you two hours or longer.

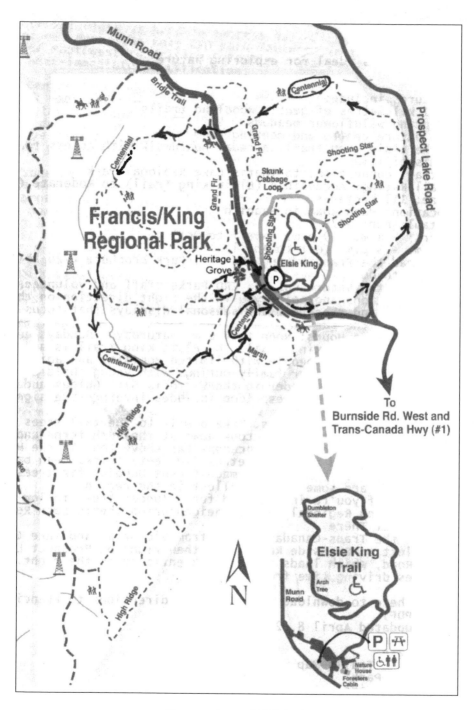

Map courtesy of CRD Parks

Trail sense
Boardwalks and other wooden crossings are slippery when wet. This is a nature appreciation park, so please keep Woofus under control at all times and clean up after.

Swimming None available

Directions to get there
Follow the Trans-Canada Highway (Douglas Street) from Victoria, and take the Helmcken Road exit. Turn left on Burnside Road West, then right on Prospect Lake Road. Keep left on Munn Road, which leads to the park entrance on the right.
🚗 25 minutes from downtown Victoria.

P 4   Mount Work, Regional Park, Victoria

Trail difficulty 🐾 🐾 - 🐾 🐾 🐾
Trail condition ☺
Time/ length 2-3 hrs.
Admission   None
Parking   Free
Hours sunrise to sunset

Restriction Dogs are prohibited from the Durrance Lake north side beach between June 1 and Sept. 15.   **Overall Rating** 🦴🦴🦴🦴

Park information

One of the largest regional parks, Mount Work Regional Park offers ideal features for a serious hike near town. Its easy to recognise feature is the highest point on the Peninsula from where one has splendid views of Victoria and the Saanich Peninsula. The variety of landscape offer a total of 11 km in hikes, and three fresh-water lakes.

There are two entrances with good parking available, one at about 40 minutes driving north from downtown and one at the south end, only about 30 minutes west from downtown.

This southern entrance, at Munns Road, has a shorter, one-hour one-way hike up to the summit. With a swim for the dog at **Fork Lake**, this can make a great afternoon of fun.

At the North end, one has the opportunity to take the dog for a shorter hike around **Durrance Lake** (see swimming below). The lake is hidden in a valley and is surrounded by forested slopes. Around the lake there is a wide, well-groomed trail from the parking lot that turns into a narrow meandering hiking trail eventually getting to a dam and back to the entrance road.that circles the lake. The south side is more like a bog with its dead trees and submerged logs.

A bit of history

Mt. Work is a corruption of Wark, which was the name of John Wark, who the park was named after. He was the Chief Factor of the Hudson's Bay Company and a member of the legislative assembly. Under the Fort Victoria Treaty, the lands were purchased from First Nations people in the mid 1800s. More than a century later, after local residents used the area for sheep grazing and selective logging, the CRD acquired the lands and established the park in 1969.

Hike Summit Trail (from the north)

The trailhead is on the east side the parking area. Shortly after you start, the initial multi-use trail splits to the right in a "hiking only" trail marked "**summit**." This leads first through thick forrest and higher, opening up to glacial rock formations. About an hour and a half hiking allong this easy to follow trail will bring you to the 446 meter summit. The trail runs north-south, reaching the park's entire length and can be challenging at times. After a number of switchbacks, a short path on the left leads to a panoramic view of Saltspring Island's **Mount Tuam**. At about 40 minutes into the hike, there is a short but steep gully to one of the several false summits that you can climb on the way. This one offers views of Saanich Inlet and accros to the **Malahat**. Go back to the main trail and keep right while climbing toward the real summit. Here, at 446 meters, the most spectacular views are towards the west, with **Mt. Finlayson, Jocelyn Hill and Lone Hill Tree Regional Park**. The Strait of Juan de Fuca and the Olympic Mountains are in the distance to the south.

Unfortunatly, there is no loop, so be prepared to take the same trail back again

.

Trail sense

Please stay on the main trails. Shortcuts damage the groundcover and with that, the eccosystem. Weather conditions can change rapidly in this area, so be prepared with good footwear and wind and raingear.

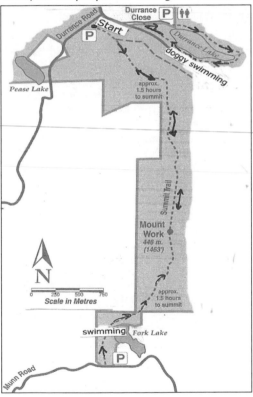

Map courtesy of CRD Parks

Swimming, Durrance Lake

The main beach area on the north side is off limmits during summer. However, if you find the narrower trail along the south side, You can both dip in for a swim in this refreshing lake any time of year.

Directions to get there

Main and Durrance Lake Entrances

From down town Victoria, take Blanshard Street north and follow the Pat Bay Highway, and take the Royal Oak Drive exit. Turn left on Royal Oak Drive to cross over the Highway, then right on West Saanich Road. Turn left on Wallace Drive, and left again on Willis Point Road. For Durrance Lake, turn right on Durrance Close, which leads to the parking lot. For the main entrance, turn left on Ross-Durrance Road, which leads to the parking lot on the left. 🚗 Allow 40 minutes from Victoria.

Fork Lake Entrance (south end)

Follow the Trans-Canada Highway from Victoria (Douglas Street) and take the Helmcken Road exit. Turn left on Burnside Road West, then right on Prospect Lake Road. Keep left on Munn Road, which leads to the parking area on the right. 🚗 Allow 30 minutes from downtown Victoria.

P 5   John Dean, Provincial Park, North Saanich

Trail difficulty 🐾 🐾 🐾
Trail condition ☺ ☹
Time/ length   1-2 hrs
Admission   none
Parking fee   free
Hours 8 am to dusk. Road access closed from Nov. – Mar.
Restrictions Dogs should be leashed.
Overall Rating 🦴🦴🦴

General Information

This 174-hectare day-use park offers a number of brisk hikes with varied degrees of difficulty and length and is within easy reach of the city. The trail winds through inspiring forest that protect one of the last stands of old-growth Douglas fir on the Peninsula. It is rather too bad that from the viewing platform near the 333 m. summit, the view over the pastoral Saanich Peninsula, to the Cascade Mountains of Washington State is quite obstructed by high-tech communications utilities. However, further down, one hikes through pristine wilderness environment with lovely creeks, ponds and marshy areas.

In First Nations culture, Mount Newton is known as Lau Wel New. For them, the mountain and surrounding areas have always been of great importance. The high point of land enabled people of the Saanich First Nations to survive the Great Flood. Legend has it that the Saanich ancestors were able to anchor their canoe with a giant cedar rope near the summit, until the floodwaters subsided.

In spring, the park comes alive with a vivid display of wildflowers native to British Columbia, including scores of blue camas lilies, which carpet the fields as well as Red Indian paintbrush, sea blush and shooting stars.

Hikes

From the parking area near the summit, walk back along the road for about 200 meters. Just over the bump, find the short trail called **Bob Boyd's Climb** on the left. Follow the steps down, and walk straight at the junction to follow **Skipper's Trail** to the Lily Pond. Here, take the stairs up to the **West Viewpoint Trail** and continue on well past **Woodward Trail**. On the left, look for **Surveyor's Trail**. Follow it over Owl Creek to some interesting viewpoints. The first is Cy's viewpoint on the right, overlooking Saanich Inlet and the Malahat beyond. Towards the southern park boundary, there is another nice lookout before the trail descends sharply via **Switchback Trail**.

Head past Canyon Creek. Here the toughest section begins. Climbing this steep section brings us to the dryer, open Garry Oak meadows. Cross **Woodward** to take **Thomson Cabin Trail** for a while. At the Y branch, take **Fern Dell Trail** if a bit more stamina remains, otherwise, take the left and follow the service road back to the parking area.

Fern Dell Trail will get you to the viewing platform at **Pickles Bluff**. Take a left at the next trail and the bluff will appear on the right where a short side trail with steps, get you to the viewpoint overlooking the Saanich Peninsula. From here, it is a short walk back to the parking area. Total distance is over 4 km of well-marked trails, but, with difficult sections.

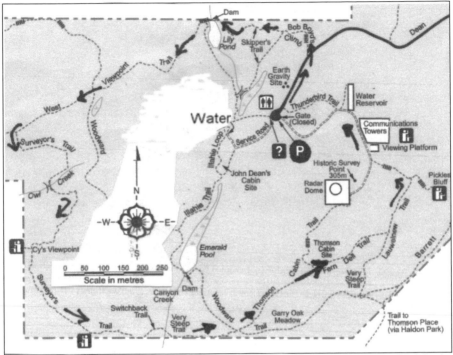

Map courtesy of BC Parks

Swimming
Not available in this park

Directions to get there
Take the Pat Bay Hwy (#17) north towards the airport and turn west onto McTavish Road, south onto East Saanich Road, then west onto John Dean Road. Follow John Dean Road until you reach the park.

🚗 approximately 35 minutes from downtown Victoria.

P 6 Gowlland Tod, Provincial Park, Highlands

Trail difficulty 🐾 - 🐾 🐾
Trail condition ☺
Time/ length <1 hr
Admission None
Parking free
Hours sunrise to sunset
Restrictions Keep dogs leashed at all times
Overall Rating 🦴🦴🦴🦴

Park information

This large park was recently established in 1994 with funds from the Commonwealth Nature Legacy to commemorate the spirit of the Commonwealth Games, held that year in Victoria. The park protects a large area of the Gowlland Range and there is about 25 km of trails in existence. It's a wilderness area, so be prepared if you attempt any of the longer hikes. The one I describe here is safe and short and can be combined with a visit to the **Butchard Gardens** nearby.

A bit of History

Over the ages, the First Nations used mainly the area around **Tod Inlet**. There must have been many Blue Grouse around at that time because they named the area 'Snitcet,' the place of blue grouse. Nowadays, one finds remnants of the Vancouver Portland Cement Company that was located at this site between 1904 and 1920.

Map courtesy of BC Parks

Hike
You start at the multi purpose trail. Shortly after, you pass via the narrow wooden crossover a sensitive land section (keep pooch on the leash). Now you can stay on the wider trail that rolls gently down to sea-level, or you can take the more challenging, but very picturesque 'hikers and dogs only' trail that follows the creek more closely down to **Tod Inlet**. The return distance is less than 3 km and can be easy accomplished within an hour unless you settle down for a picnic at one of the tables provided.

Trail sense
By staying on the trail, you help to protect the sensitive habitat.

Swimming
Tod Inlet is a quiet and protected salt-water inlet. Jump in if you feel like it.

Directions to get there
Take Blanshard Street north and follow Highway 17 until Keating Cross Road. Turn left off the highway. Follow this road to the end, continue straight onto Benvenuto Ave and turn left on Wallace Drive. Watch for the the park entrance on the right.

🚗 approximately 35 minutes from Victoria.

P 7   Coles Bay Regional Park, North Saanich

Trail difficulty   🐾 - 🐾🐾
Trail condition   ☺
Time/ length   20 min.
Admission   None
Parking   Free
Hours dawn to dusk

Restrictions Dogs must be leashed when passing through picnic and beach areas and are not allowed to stay between June 1 and Sept. 15.

Overall Rating 🦴🦴🦴🦴

Park information

This is a small park with a great attraction. It is the lovely south facing beach overlooking Saanich inlet and the Malahat to the west that draws us here.

There are two trails. The quickest way to the beach is **Beach Trail**. It leaves from the mid section of the parking lot and is easy for everyone. Exploring the beach and tidal lagoon can take as long as you want here because your return trail is not much longer than the way you came. Towards the Westside along the beach, you will find the return trail, called **Nature Trail.** It is nicer, hillier and winds through western red cedar, broadleaf maple and Douglas fir forest. It crosses the creek and reaches the parking lot by the regular pit-toilets. Without a stop at the beach, you can walk the loop in 20 minutes.

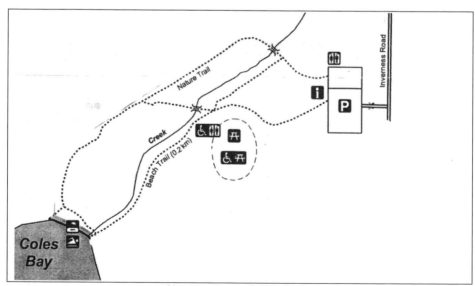

Map courtesy of CRD Parks

A bit of history
The park was established in 1966 and is named after John Coles. He was a midshipman aboard HMS Thetis, and visited this bay first in 1851.

Trail sense
Stairs at the beach can be troublesome. Keep the dog on the leash when other people are sunbathing. Go beyond and take Pooch for a run at low tide.

Swimming
A gentle, mostly protected beach with pebble, mud and rock provides excellent swimming. The water warms up most during ebbing.

Bonus
The first, short part of the **Beach Trail** is wheelchair accessible, to reach the picnic area and wheelchair accessible toilets.

Directions to get there
Follow the Pat Bay Highway (# 17) from Victoria, (Blanshard Street in town) to McTavis Road where you turn left. This is the same exit used to go to the airport, however stay on McTavish untill West Saanich Rd. (a golf course is on your right) Take a right turn for one block and turn left onto Ardmore Drive. Turn left again onto Inverness Road. Here you will see the parkinglot on your right.

Allow 30 minutes from downtown Victoria.

From the Swartz Bay Ferry, it's only 15 minutes. Follow the highway south past Sidney and turn right at McTavish and follow directions above.

P 8 Sidney Spit, Provincial Marine Park, Sidney Island

Trail difficulty   🐾

Trail condition   ☺

Time/ length 1- 3 hrs

Admission see foot-passenger ferry info below

Parking fee   Yes

Hours see ferry schedule

Restrictions Dogs should be leashed

Overall Rating 🦴🦴🦴🦴🦴

General Information
This is a beautiful marine park that is easy accessible for boat and non-boat owners. There is sheltered anchorage on the west side of the spit. The foot passenger ferry from Sidney (see for fares and schedule below) uses the wharf and landing floats for small craft. A twenty-minute boat ride will get you to white sandy beaches with towering bluffs, scenic tidal flats and salt marshes crowded with birds, mammals and marine life. It is hard to believe that all these outdoor wonders are so close to city and airport.

Hike
From the public wharf, go up the bluff and enjoy the views. East, Mt. Baker will be in view on a clear day, while west and northwards Vancouver Island and Saltspring will be visible during most weather conditions. At this point, you should look at the condition of the tide and decide to hike the Spit first, or wait for lower water to get better conditions for beachcombing along that side.

From here, there is a nice trail following the east side of the island taking you a little over two kilometers along the shore. Wonderfully shaped Arbutus trees make the first part very attractive. Further out, a large grassy area awaits, where you walk around clockwise. The many deer always excite our dog and extensive sniffing here usually slows us down quite a bit. If you have the time, walk west towards to the interesting tidal flats. Here you can hike another two-kilometer peninsula called the Claw.

Remember that it is still six km back to your ferry. You would not want to miss the last ferry back to Sidney without some provisions for the night ahead.

Swimming
Thousands of meters of sandy shoreline provide excellent swimming on the inside of the spit where the water also tends to warm up at times during the summer.

Bonus

A large hand pump near the dock provides drinking water for your pet.

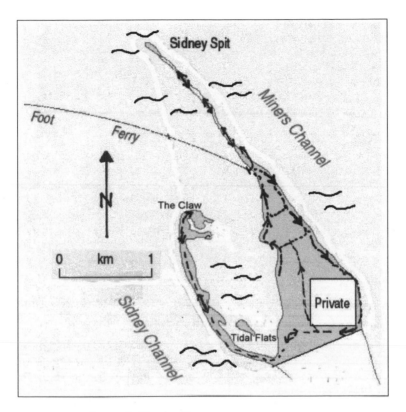

Foot-passenger ferry information

Adult tickets are $ 11.00 for a return trip. Discounts for Seniors and children. Children under two and dogs travel free.

From mid-May to the end of September, the ferry leaves on the hour between 10 am and 6 pm, Fridays and Saturdays. The ferry runs only until 5pm on Sundays. From the end of June to the beginning of September the ferry also runs weekdays 10-5. Call 250-474-5145 to confirm.

Directions to get there

Take the Pat Bay Hwy (#17) north to Sidney and turn right at McTavish Rd. (the Airport exit is left) Follow Lochside Drive left going north along the water. Continue straight into the town of Sidney and turn right at Beacon Avenue. Start to look for parking; it's only a few blocks to the foot of Beacon Ave., from where the ferry leaves.

🚗 approximately 30minutes from Victoria to the footpassenger ferry.

P 9   Cordova Spit, Central Saanich

Trail difficulty 🐾
Trail condition ☺
Time/ length < 1 hr
Admission   None
Parking   Free
Hours dawn to dusk
Restrictions Respect hiking on First Nations Land
Overall Rating 🦴🦴🦴🦴

Park information
Cordova Spit is made of all the sediments washed along the beach and is mostly flat with sparse vegetation. On the western side is a large marshy area that can be quite wet during high tides. The best time to hike the shoreline is on a falling tide. The fresh exposed hard sand is a joy to walk on! This is one of the quietest beaches in the Greater Victoria area, so enjoy.
The spit is very open to the elements. Incredible scenery surrounds you in every direction you look. If you'd like to make the walk into a hike, find the shoreline. Walking west to east, counter clockwise, makes you believe that the high bluffs of James Island, about half a mile away, are part of the spit. In the center of the spit are a few eroded road paths that are easy to walk. The total perimeter of the spit is sure to tire you and your furry companion. **Look for the map on page 63.**
Total time around can take up to an hour. That's without splashing in the ocean and sniffing everything out between the huge piles of driftwood.

A bit of history
Cordova Spit is the geological offspring of nearby **Island View Beach Regional Park** (see there), a high ridge to the south. Several ice sheets that covered southern Vancouver Island as recently as ten thousand years ago shaped this area. Thousands of years of wave action since then, have eroded the ridge, depositing the sediments along the shore to give Cordova Spit its classic shape.
The whole area falls under a historic treaty agreement that the Tsawout First Nations signed with Governor James Douglas in 1852. This treaty effectively abolished aboriginal title to those nations that signed them, but also promised to allow those indigenous peoples to carry on their fisheries and other hunting activities as they formerly had, for millennia to come.

Trail sense
Respect the First Nations rights to the lands resources. If you don't want your dog to get wet or dirty, keep the leash handy.
Walk this area at your own discretion; try to ask permission on your way in if you see someone.

60

Jazz with my wife Marianne at Cordova Spit in spring

Swimming
This is one of the best spots for canine swimming, without a doubt. Depending on the time of year, this is an excellent spot for both, you and your dog.

Bonus
The variety of land nearby as well as the Cordova channel attracts a large variety of shore birds and waterfowl. This makes the spit a bird watching paradise in three out of four seasons.

Directions to get there, (Look for map on next page)
Follow the Pat Bay Highway (# 17) from Victoria, (Blanshard Street in town). Turn right at the lights at McDonalds. This is Mt. Newton Cross Road, follow this to the waterside where you turn right and keep left until the end. Sometimes it is possible to ask permission at the band office on the way in. Another option is to go to the campground. They lease the land from the band, and ask if you can park there.

🚗 Allow 25 minutes from downtown Victoria, or 15 minutes from the Swartz Bay Ferry.

P 10 Island View Beach, Regional Park, Central Saanich

Trail difficulty 🐾
Trail condition ☺
Time/ length 2 km
Admission None
Parking Free
Hours dawn to dusk

Restrictions Dogs must be leashed when passing through beach and picnic areas and are not allowed to stay there from June 1 to   Sep. 15.

Overall Rating 🦴🦴🦴🦴

Park information

This is a relatively small park, but has a lot to offer with its panoramic seascapes over Cordova Channel towards James and Sidney Islands. The best part is the long sandy beach for Pooch, be it only outside summer restriction time to enjoy. But on a very low tide, at any time of year, one can start at the boat-ramp and hike the beach for 10 km if you like, all the way south to **Mt. Douglas Park** (see there).

A bit of history

After the ice age, this area was shaped by the retrieving icecap leaving ridges called 'drumlins.' You see them on James and Sidney Island and on the Peninsula to the west. Saanich People lived along these shorelines for centuries and still own much of the land north and west of this park.

Hike

You can do a **circle hike**. When you reach the end of Island View Road, there is a boat ramp where you turn left for the first parking lot that has toilets that could come in handy. Two hundred meters further is another parking lot. At the beginning on the right, follow the path down to the beach, and continue through the dunes, but stay on the trail. About 200 meters before the end of the park, there is a path to the left, which leads inland through back-dunes and salt marsh.

At a low tide, one can make a longer hike by starting at the boat ramp, walk below the high-tide line past the few private homes, and go as far as the beach and sandbar is exposed.

Trail sense

Keep your dog at close range and have him not chase or harass the migrating birds. They are tired and need to forage and rest here before they can continue their long journeys.

The park's northern boundary adjoins the East Saanich Indian Reserve. Walk this area at your own discretion; there is nowhere to ask permission at the time of writing.

Swimming

Depending on the time of year, this is an excellent spot for both, you and the dog. Jazz, our retriever, can fish here for hours if the current is not too strong.

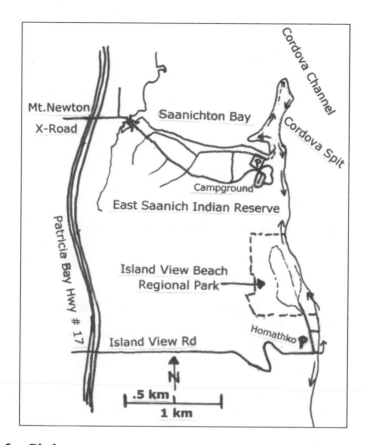

Bonus for Birders

Island View is a park used much by migrating birds. In winter, look at the waters in the channel for four species of loons: Common Loons are regular, and Red-throated Loons sometimes feed only a few feet off the beach. Pacific Loons are regular through the winter, and increase in numbers greatly in late winter and spring. Yellow-billed Loon is a possibility in winter. Red-necked and Horned Grebes are the most common, with Western being irregular here, and Eared Grebe uncommon.

Directions to get there

Follow the Pat Bay Highway (# 17) from Victoria, (Blanshard Street in town). Turn right on Island View Road, then left on Homathko Road, which leads to the park entrance.

🚗 Allow 25 minutes from downtown Victoria, or 15 minutes from the Swartz Bay Ferry.

P 11   Mount Douglas Park, East Saanich

Trail difficulty   🐾 🐾
Trail condition   ☺ ☹
Time/ length 1-2 hrs
Admission   None
Parking   Free
Hours Dawn to Dusk
Restrictions Dogs are not allowed in beach or picnic area
from May 1 to August 31
Overall Rating 🦴🦴🦴🦴

Park information
With a summit of 277 meters, Mount Doug as it is known locally is the highest point in the urban Victoria area. Yet still, if you walk the trails under the high canopy of the huge trees, you get the sense of being far out of town and definitely on the west coast.

Hike
From the large parking lot, take the **Merriman Trail** at the end of the lot. It crosses the road and turns right around a **quarry** on the left. Start the ascent and when you are close to the road that goes to the summit, cross it and take the **Irvine Trail** to the top parking lot. Here is a short but steep **Summit Trail** that will reward you with fabulous views in all directions.
Another option is to take the **Irvine Trail** from across the entrance road of the parking lot. A short detour will get you to **Irvine Hill**, which has a nice viewpoint over Cordova Bay and beyond.
In both cases, allow yourself about an hour for the way up. With some time at the top, the whole hike could take a couple of hours. For variety, use one trail up and the other down.
There are many more trails in this park, some of which are at the west side and are very steep at places.

A bit of history
In the early days, this mountain was called "hill of cedars" and noticeably covered with them. After most of the first growth was harvested to be used as fortification for Fort Victoria, the cartographer at the time named it after the Governor, James Douglas.

Trail sense
Stay on the trails, making shortcuts erodes the park.

Swimming
At low tide, there is a huge beach down from the steps at the end of a short path. It starts to the right from the picnic area below Cordova Bay Road.

Directions to get there

From downtown Victoria, take Douglas Street north to Hillside. Turn right and go all the way to the corner of the Hillside Mall. Here at the lights you take a left on to Shelbourne, which will get you all the way to the park.
It's about 8 km. 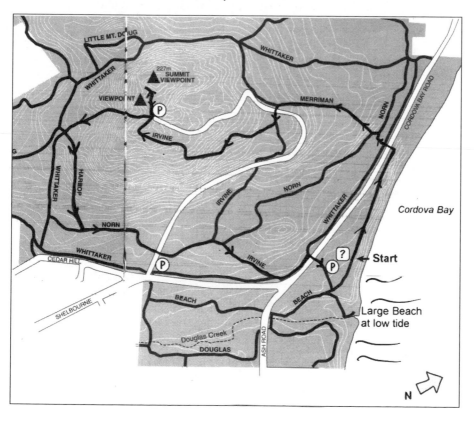 allow yourself about 20 minutes.

From the north, into town by Highway # 1, turn left at McKenzie, follow this to Shelbourne and turn left again.

From the Swartz Bay Ferry, Highway # 17 south and take the Royal Oak exit. Turn left and drive until the end where at the lights go strait onto Cordova Bay Road. This will turn right while the ocean will show up on your left. Watch for the large parking lot coming up on the left.
Allow 20 minutes from the ferry.

Map courtesy of Saanich Parks

Cuthbert Holmes Park, Saanich, has great running areas

Esquimalt Lagoon, good running

French Beach Provincial Park, simply beautiful

McKenzie Bight, trail and beach, both are nice

Nanaimo River, Park and trails are great

Portland Island, so serene

Rithet's Bog in Broadmead is a nice walk

Ruckle Park, Saltspring Isl.

Mystic Vale/Henderson Field near U.Vic is very popular.
This are Henry and Robinson near the 'Lost & Found' pole

Locater Map, Western Section

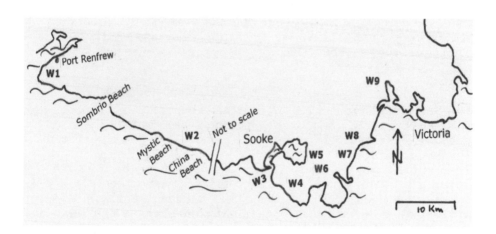

W 1 **Botanical Beach,** Provincial Park, Port Renfrew

Trail difficulty 🐾 🐾
Trail condition ☺
Time/ length 2 hrs
Admission None
Parking $ 1.00 -$ 5.00
Hours sunrise to sunset
Restrictions Keep dogs leashed at all times.
Overall Rating 🦴🦴🦴🦴🦴

Park information

Botanical Beach is part of the large **Juan de Fuca Park** and is at the far western part of the trail. It is out of the way, but worth the trip if you plan to be there at the right time. This is at about a tide of one meter or less. Consult tide tables and be aware to ad one hour during daylight savings time.

The beach is for the most part a massive flat rock formation and is one of the richest inter-tidal areas along the west coast. The shoreline has unique ridges of shale and quartz, which jut up through the black basalt forming huge tableaus with many tidal-pools. Watching the fascinating marine life in the tidal pools is only possible at low tide. From March to April, a large number of Grey whales, migrating from Mexico to Alaska, might be seen feeding off the nearby points.

Park authorities are not kidding with the numerous warnings about bears here. During our last visit in June, we had a pleasant confrontation with two of the burly creatures. They went their way and we went ours. No problems if you use a bear-bell.

Hikes

The **Botanical Loop** is a 2.5 km trail that when taken counterclockwise, reaches **Botany Bay** first. Worthwhile for a visit. Back to the trail, you get several beach access points to the right that makes it hard to resist wandering off.

Keep in mind that there are orange balls hanging on the trees marking your point of return in case the tide cuts you off any other way. Thanks to the many boardwalk sections, the muddy areas are minimal. **WARNING, be aware that occasional rogue waves can flush you or your dog of the rocky surface with disastrous consequences.** A second trail, short but steep down to **Mill Bay**, leaves a parking lot beside the road to Botanical Beach. Here a small pebble and shell beach can be enjoyed in a more protected area on windy days.

Trail sense

Impact of human activity on the intertidal area is of growing concern. When visiting Botanical Beach, please look in the tide pools only, do not touch, remove or disturb the marine life. This is all part of a vulnerable ecosystem that Botanical Beach was established to protect.

Swimming

There are no designated areas for swimming, however, **Botany Bay** offers some protection and would be suitable on a calm day.

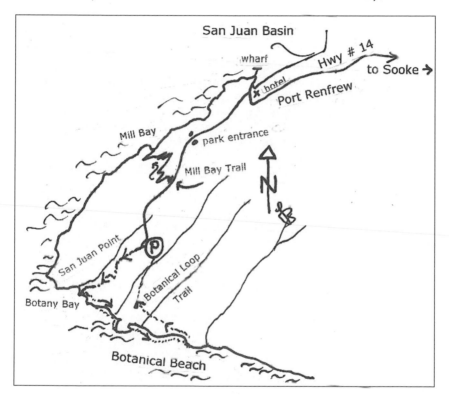

Directions to get there

Take Douglas Street and follow the Trans-Canada Highway # 1 from Victoria to Colwood. Take the exit to Sooke, which is Highway # 14 and follow this all the way to Port Renfrew (72 km from Sooke) and turn left to the park entrance which is a few more km over gravel.

🚗 Approximately 2 hours from Victoria.

W 2   China Beach, Provincial Park, Jordan River

Trail difficulty   🐾 - 🐾🐾
Trail condition   ☺
Time/ length 1 -2 hrs
Admission   None
Parking $ 1.00 - $ 5.00
Hours sunrise to sunset
Restrictions Keep dogs leashed at all times
Overall Rating 🦴🦴🦴🦴🦴

Park information

Typical west coast scenery awaits you at the east end and start of the Juan de Fuca hiking trail. This trail is a recent addition to accommodate the overload of the famous West Coast Trail, which is much further along the coast. Bring your own water. Tide tables come in handy as well. They are usually posted at the trailheads, and be aware to add one hour during daylight savings time.

Hikes

An impressive, 1 km trail leads from the parking lot south through giant, moss-covered trees to the beach. Notice the sounds of the swells building the closer you get to this spectacular beach.

On the way down, a large deck offers majestic views of the beach and the Juan de Fuca Strait. This is an easy to moderate, partly steep trail. Once on the beach, you could hike west towards a waterfall, or east as far as the beach allows. Keep in mind that orange balls on the trees indicate your escape route back in case a sudden high tide or bad weather surprises you.

Another, longer trail leads westward from the parking area through magnificent old forest to **Mystic Beach**. This is part of the **Juan de Fuca Trail** and is over 2km one way, using a suspension bridge over Pete Wolfe Creek. Take more than one hour for your return trip to spend some time on this truly 'mystic' beach.

China Beach to Mystic Beach Trail

Trail sense
Don't take short cuts and keep the dog on the leash while on the trail.

Swimming
On calm days, China and Mystic beach offer wonderful sandy beach swimming. Watch out for a common strong undertow.

Directions to get there
Take Douglas Street and follow the Trans-Canada Highway from Victoria to Colwood where you take the exit to Sooke. Follow Highway # 14. From the first bridge past Jordan River, it is only a few kilometers to the China Beach day-use area on the left. (second China Beach sign)
Approximately 1.5 hours from Victoria.

W 3   Whiffin Spit, Sooke

Trail difficulty 🐾
Trail condition ☺
Time/ length 1-2 hrs
Admission   None
Parking   Free
Hours   dawn-dusk
Restrictions Dogs should always be under control
Overall Rating 🦴🦴🦴🦴

Hike information

The spit is much longer than you expect, while the magic Olympic Mountains seem to be much closer then they really are. Altogether, this spit is a wonderful spot for an hour or two wandering the shorelines and observing shore birds and playful seals nearby.
If one is interested in fine art, exquisite herbs or delicate edible flowers, the world-renowned 'Sooke Harbour House,' just before the spit is worth a visit.
Some giant woodcarvings are displayed near the beginning of the spit.

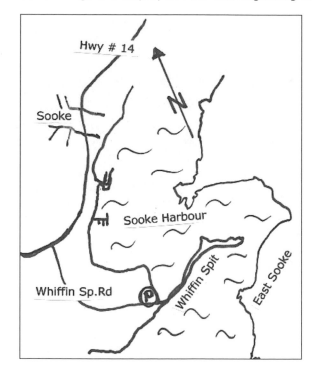

A bit of history
The spit is named after John George Whiffin. He was a clerk aboard the HMS 'Herald', a Royal Navy vessel in 1846.

Trail sense
Keep Rover away from the often tired, feeding migrating birds.

Swimming
On either side of the long spit are shallow areas where dogs love to venture Into the ocean. Don't swim at the end of the spit. The strong current here is dangerous.

Directions to get there
From Victoria, take Douglas Street north and follow Highway # 1 to the Colwood exit. Once you underpass the highway, you are on Sooke Road, which is Highway # 14. Follow this road into Sooke village. From here it is another 2 km on the West Coast Road untill you see Whiffen Spit Road on the left and follow to the end.

🚗 Allow 50 minutes from Victoria.

Giant woodcarvings near Whiffin Spit

W 4   East Sooke Regional Park, East Sooke

Trail difficulty 🐾🐾 - 🐾🐾🐾
Trail condition ☺- ☹
Time/ length 2-6 hrs
Admission   None
Parking   Free
Hours Down to Dusk

Restrictions Dogs are prohibited from Aylard Farm pond –all year and from Aylard Farm beach and picnic area between June 1 and Sept. 15.

Overall Rating 🦴🦴🦴🦴🦴

Park information

If you want a taste of true West Coast wilderness within an hours drive from Victoria, this is your park. When you hike along the windswept rocky coast, over the hilltops, and through dark rainforest to sheltered coves the experience is breathtaking. This I mean both ways, figuratively and literally. Beautiful vistas, possible wildlife encounters and last but not least, the sheer distance and tiresome climbs. The park totals more than 50 km. of trails, from a simple one hour to strenuous six or eight hours with some spectacular views of the Strait of Juan de Fuca and the Olympic Mountains.

Hikes from one of three entry points

From **Aylard Farm** it is a 5-minute walk through the old orchard and open fields to a concave beach where intertidal life and river otters can be discovered. Follow the shoreline right, to **Alldridge Point,** where some interesting Petroglyphs can be found. This will take about 20 to 30 minutes. Follow the red-tagged trail. You can take a shortcutting trail back from here to the parking lot or continue onto **Beechey Head** (1 hour total) and take the interior trail back to the parking. This return trail will be shorter, keeping your hike under two hours.

Anderson Cove, on Sooke Basin, is a good starting point for hiking to **Babbington Hill**. On this 228 meter summit, you might see Bald eagles, vultures, and red-tailed hawks hunting for prey. If not, you will at least be rewarded with panoramic views of the Olympic Peninsula. Trail time is about two hours one way.

Pike Road is the westerly access to the park, and to the demanding **Coast Trail**. Follow the old logging road that leads through forest and meadows to the beach at **Iron Mine Bay**. An interesting variety of periwinkles, goose neck barnacles and purple sea star can be found in the intertidal zonne at low tide. Please, only take pictures! Trail time to the shelter is only about half an hour. One can wander to **Pike Point** and back or follow the Coast Trail briefly and then take a left back through the interior. A second left will bring you back to the Pike Road logging trail. Total time is about 1.5 hours.

For the adventurous, there is the complete rugged **Coast Trail.** In hiking circles, East Sooke's **Coast Trail** is considered one of the best wilderness

74

day-hikes within easy reach of a city. This is a 10 km snaking trail through rugged and uneven terrain. It is a challenging 6 - 8 hour hike even for expert hikers. A pickup should be arranged at one point and bring plenty of water and first aid equipment.

Trail sense
This is a wilderness park. Be prepared to encounter deer, black bear or cougars. Do not have your dog stray away and keep her under control at all time.

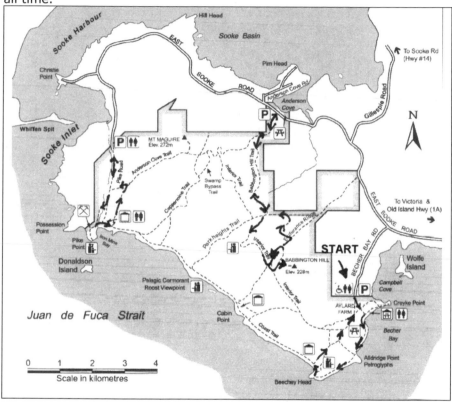

Map courtesy of CRD Parks

Swimming
Some spots along the **Coast Trail** are suitable for a dip, but the nicest spot is **Anderson Cove**.

Directions to get there
Take Douglas Street north and follow the Trans-Canada Highway (# 1) from Victoria, and take the Colwood exit. Follow the Old Island Highway, which turns into Sooke Road. From Sooke Road (Hwy # 14), turn left on Gillespie Road. Turn right on East Sooke Road to reach the entrances at **Anderson Cove** and **Pike Road**, or turn left to reach the park entrance at **Aylard Farm (**off Becher Bay Road). 🚗 1 hour from Victoria.

W 5   Roche Cove Regional Park, East Sooke

Trail difficulty 🐾 - 🐾🐾
Trail condition ☺ - ☹
Time/ length 1-2 hrs
Admission   None
Parking   Free
Hours Down to Dusk
Restrictions Dogs must be leashed when passing through beach and picnic areas and are not allowed to stay there from June 1- Sept. 15
Overall Rating 🦴🦴🦴🦴

Park information

Roche Cove is connected to the ocean and has large tidal fluctuations daily. You can see a strong current from the bridge where Gillespie Road crosses the narrow opening into the much larger Sooke Basin. A steep rock-face guides the water inland to the protected cove where, on a muddy bottom, blue mussels and littleneck clams can be found at low tide. The quiet waters give shelter to ducks, when the larger basin is wild and choppy. Sea stars move in during high tide and you can see them looking for food on underwater rocks and broken shells.

A large part of the 163 hectares is north of the famous **Galloping Goose Trail** that cuts right through this park. Roche Cove Park is directly adjacent **Matheson Lake Regional Park** (see there). Hikes can easily be combined with this neighboring park and other parts of the **Galloping Goose Trail**.

Cedar Grove Hike

From the parking lot, find the trailhead to north side of the lot, before you reach the pit toilets and picnic tables. The trail follows a reasonable climb along dry, rocky outcrops into a profuse temperate rainforest. The trail is easy to follow, down through large big-leaf maples. While your dog will enjoy all the new scents around these giant trees, make sure you look up into the canopy of the forest. It is a different world out there with its own astonishing microcosm of lichens, ferns and mosses.

Shortly after, you will head uphill again. There is a sign pointing to a viewpoint to the right of which not much is left. It is as if the trees here have been on steroids, everything is gigantic and overgrown. When hiking north, take the first fork to the right and in about 15 minutes you walk by a giant cedar that has come down after 500 years.

Past this cedar grove, the trail gets harder to follow. On the left, you will pass an alder forest with bird life active here half the year. When you follow the trail from here, it will start to descend and reach the **Galloping Goose Trail**. To the right on this trail, you can enjoy the easy flat part of this hike back to the parking lot. There is a small detour of about 10 minutes, if you like, to a nice viewpoint at Roche Cove when you follow the sign. This part of the trail takes you up through forest

76

again and eventually loops back to the **Goose Trail**. Before you reach the parking lot, on your left are some stunning views of the cove.

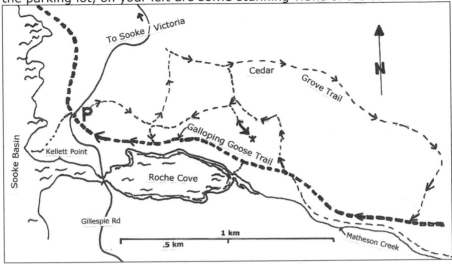

Map courtesy of CRD Parks

Trail Time
The Cedar Grove hike can take approximately 2 hours and is definitely the more invigorating type since the elevation varies much of the time. Another hike is along Roche Cove, following Matheson Creek up to the lake at **Matheson Regional Park** (see W6). A return hike is between 7 and 8 kilometers and can take over 2 hours.

The easiest terrain is the wide, level and mostly gravel surfaced **Galloping Goose Trail** section that cuts through the park from the parking lot.

Trail sense
Like everywhere else in the Capital Regional District Parks, the recommendations are to have your dog leashed if your dog does not obey well. Keep dogs on the trail and remove droppings!, it will be so much appreciated by visitors behind you.

Swimming
Yes, it is available in the cove.

Bonus
A short path across Gillespie Road and the parking lot leads to **Kellett Point**, a beautiful lookout over the wide expanse of Sooke Basin, a great spot for a picnic.

Directions to get there
Follow the Trans-Canada Highway from Victoria, and take the Colwood exit. Follow the Old Island Highway, which turns into Sooke Road. From Sooke Road, turn left on Gillespie Road, which leads to the park entrance on the left. 🚗 Approximately 45 minutes from Victoria.

W 6   Matheson Lake Regional Park, East Sooke

Trail difficulty 🐾 🐾
Trail condition ☺
Time/ length   1 hr.+
Admission   None
Parking   Free
Hours   Dawn to Dusk
Restrictions No dogs in picnic and beach areas from June 1- Sept. 15
Overall Rating 🦴🦴🦴🦴

Park information

Matheson Lake Park is 157 hectares and borders part of **The Galloping Goose Trail.** The park is easily accessible yet you feel you are somewhere remote on the west coast with some old-growth forest, many varieties of mosses, rock formations and above all, a beautiful lake to dip in on a hot summer's day.
Hikes can easily be combined with neighboring **Roche Cove Regional Park** (see W5) and other parts of the famous Galloping Goose Trail.

Hikes

From the parking lot, a quiet hike runs clock-wise around the lake. It allows you to stay close to the lake most of the time.
At the top-end of the lake you can leave the water for a different hike in the dry season. It follows the creek out from the lake, going west to **Roche Cove**.
Another option is at the north side of the lake to go up to the Galloping Goose Trail and follow it east for a few kilometers following the flat and wide trail to Rocky Point Road. Turn right and the next road right again brings you back to the parking lot at the entrance of **Matheson Lake Park.**

Trail Time and condition

The loop around the lake is about 4 km and can take you less than an hour. If you continue on to **Roche Cove**, the distance is about 4 km one way. Going east along the **Galloping Goose** to Rocky Point Rd. and back to the parking lot makes a 7 km circle (partly on blacktop)

In dry conditions, the terrain can still be challenging due to the various ups and downs. After rain, some of the trail can get slippery and muddy. Gravel, rock and moss make up the surface of most of the lake-loop trail. The **Galloping Goose** section is easy, flat and mostly gravel or sand.

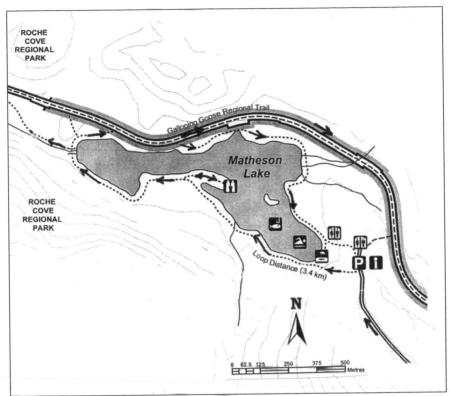

Map courtesy of CRD Parks

Trail sense

Keep the dog on the trail and if your dog does not obey well, keep it leashed to avoid confrontation with other wildlife of which there is plenty out here. Removing droppings from the trail would be much appreciated by park visitors that follow after you.

Swimming

Is allowed all year, but you cannot have your dog at the sandy beach/ picnic area from June 1 to September 15. At that time, use other lake access points.

Directions to get there

Follow the Trans-Canada Highway from Victoria, and take the Colwood exit. Follow the Old Island Highway, which turns into Sooke Road. From Sooke Road, turn left on Happy Valley Road, then right on Rocky Point Road, and right again on Matheson Lake Park Road, which leads to the park entrance.

🚗 Approximately 40 minutes from Victoria.

W7 Devonian Regional Park, Metchosin

Trail difficulty 🐾 - 🐾 🐾
Trail condition ☺
Time/ length 2 km +
Admission None
Parking Free
Hours Down to Dusk
Restrictions Dogs should be under control and are prohibited from Sherwood Creek.
Overall Rating 🦴🦴🦴🦴

Park information

This is a relatively new park, established in 1980. One can only imagine that the neighboring pastoral lands are just waiting to be bought up and joined to the larger Witty's Lagoon Park, a few kilometers to the north, if the Capital Region had the money.

The park by itself is small, 14.4 hectares, however, combined with a hike along the beach when the tide is low, to Witty's Lagoon, can make an especially varied full circle hike of about 8 or 9 kilometers (3 km along the road).

The Beach Trail

From the parking lot, it is only a few hundred meters before you get the choice of two routes. You could stay north of the Sherwood creek for a while or go to the left, and down to cross the creek early and follow it along a nice wide fir-needle covered trail called '**Beach Trail**.' At spots, it gets narrower and leads up and down, following the creek to Sherwood Pond.

This last part is rocky and follows the dried up area of the pond before you reach Parry Bay, which has a picturesque cobble beach. Large pieces of driftwood offer a great spot for a picnic or to rest on and to take-in the majestic views on clear days. The views reach from Washington State's Olympic Mountains with William Head in front, and if you are lucky, Mount Baker towering above Victoria to the northeast. You can take a different trail back. This trail is to the left and is shared with horseback riders.

Trail Time and condition

The return trail is just over 2 kilometers, but I am sure you'll stop at the beach rather than hiking non-stop. The beach is simply too nice. So the actual time depends on how long your stop at the beach is.

The mostly shaded **Beach Trail** is ideal for hot sunny days. Needles from Douglas fir keep the trail soft. The balance of the forested area is broadleaf maple. There are some elevation differences, but nothing serious. Devonian is a lovely quiet park with good bird watching at the pond. Watch out for the swans.

80

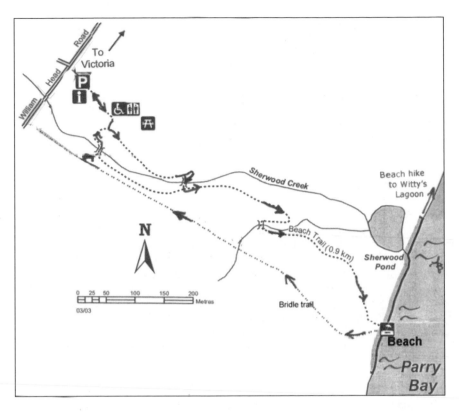

Map courtesy or CRD Parks

Trail sense
Do not disturb the creek. It has a fragile habitat and is host to trout spawning from October to March.

Swimming
At the beach, for sure, but do not let the dog get into the pond. Its small and the waterfowl would 'have a bird.'

Directions to get there
Follow the Trans-Canada Highway from Victoria, and take the Colwood exit. Follow the Old Island Highway (# 14) which turns into Sooke Road. From Sooke Road, turn left on Metchosin Road, which turns into William Head Road at the Happy Valley Road junction. Follow William Head Road to the park entrance on the left.

🚗 approximately 40 minutes from Victoria.

W 8   Witty's Lagoon Regional Park, Metchosin

Trail difficulty 🐾 - 🐾🐾
Trail condition ☺ - ☹
Time/ length   5 km +
Admission   Free
Parking   Free
Hours 8 a.m. to sunset
Restrictions No dogs in picnic or beach areas from June 1 to Sept.15
Overall Rating 🦴🦴🦴🦴🦴

Park information and history

The diversity of this park, its ease of access and scenery makes hiking around Witty's Lagoon one of my favorites. 56 Hectares are divided in about three different accessible areas.

Shell middens have revealed ancient fishing and other tools used by Salish Indians of the Northern Straits. In the nineteenth century, members of the Ka Kyaakan band inhabited the site. After James Douglas of the Hudson Bay Company purchased all the land in the area, a settler's community developed. In 1867 a **Mr. John Witty** became owner of the property and the band members were allowed to stay to provide transport to Fort Victoria by dugout canoe.

In 1966, the CRD Parks obtained the first 18 hectares and started preserving a unique ecosystem that is very special to hike through.

Hikes

The smallest is an easy 20 minutes walk that takes you around **Tower Point** following **Rocky Bluff Trail**. Fantastic views show the drying rocks in Parry Bay with dozens of sea lions and seals and a large sandy beach at low tide. The grassy field here is a perfect running area for Max as long as you keep him out of the picnic area. Even when the ocean is white capping from winds of 15 to 20 knots straight into this area, you can still have a quiet picnic behind a protecting band of bush.

A short trail leads down to a small beach at **Tower Point** where the constant pounding of ocean waves have hollowed tide pools in the granite outcropping.

At low tide, one can cross the lagoon outlet to the large beach at the other side and make this into a longer, circular hike.

The largest section of the park is in the middle and is wheelchair accessible. The **Lagoon Trail** in this section is about 25 minutes one way.

The most spectacular trail is direct from the main parking lot keeping left. It is the **Beach Trail** and is a bit more difficult but very rewarding. Soon after the start, you will hear the rush of **Sitting Lady Falls** plunging into the lagoon below. The mixture of salt and fresh water attracts a large variety of waterfowl. Kingfishers rattle; juncos and warblers sing further down in the forest. The trail winds down soon to ocean level. Before you reach the beach, there is a large salty intertidal marsh in front of the sand spit.

From the beach, you can have lunch and watch the seals and otters play and feed in the kelp-bed a few hundred yards out. This is a vantage point from which on a clear day, you can look across the Strait to the towering heights of the Olympic Mountains in Washington State and its Hurricane Ridge formation.

To the south is another access point to this beach with free parking. The steps here are steep and feel endless. If you like to make this hike into a longer, 9 km hike, check the tides and if low, you can walk 3 km. along the beach to **Devonlan Regional Park** (see W7) and back along the road to 'recharge' at the cozy "My-Chosen Café."

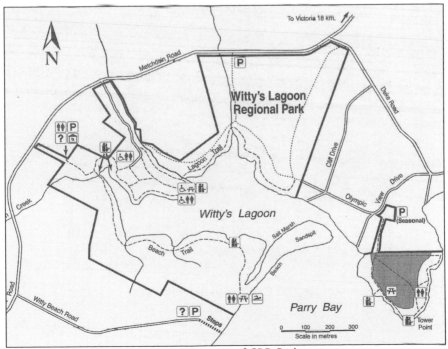

Map Courtesy of CRD Parks

Trail sense

This can be a busy park and with many ducks and other waterfowl in the marshy area, keep your dog close and out of the picnic areas. Don't trample the abundance of wildflowers at the meadow near the main entrance and at Tower Point

Swimming

Yes, you can swim at the beach, both of you, if you like. Its gradually dropping sandy beach can warm up nicely during a low tide. It is not a good idea to swim in the lagoon.

Directions to get there

Main Entrance Follow the Trans-Canada Highway from Victoria, and take the Colwood exit. Follow the Old Island Highway, which turns into Sooke Road. From Sooke Road, turn left on Metchosin Road, which leads to the park entrances on the left.

🚗 about 35 minutes from Victoria.

Tower Point Entrance

From Metchosin Road, turn left on Duke Road, then right on Olympic View Drive, which leads to the parking area on the left.

Members of 'Trail Blazers' walking the beach in spring

Mill Hill Regional Park, Langford

Trail difficulty 🐾 - 🐾 🐾
Trail condition ☺
Time/ length 40 min.3 km
Admission None
Parking Free

Hours 8 a.m. – 8 p.m. April to October, 8am- 5pm October to April
Restrictions A proposal is underway to make this an 'on-leash' park

Overall Rating 🦴🦴🦴

Park information and history

Millstream Creek follows the south boundary of the park and is the most densely forested. Mill Hill itself is a rocky hilltop, and in between the hill and the forested area is open woodland with Arbutus and Garry Oak.

Findings at an archeological site in the park have indicated that the Songhees people camped here, where they used spears to catch salmon in Millstream Creek some 2500 years ago. The finding of harpoon tips confuses the matter and one assumes that they were used to hunt deer or beavers. The Hudson Bay Company was an eager buyer of the supply of beaver skins.

The creek has a historic importance in B.C. since it powered the first lumber mill ever built in the province. By 1855, steam technology made this mill obsolete. After several private owners, the lands became Dominion property. On top of the hill was a lookout tower to locate forest fires. In 1976, the lands were leased as a public park and in 1981, the CRD Parks took over the park and now has its head offices next to the parking lot.

Hikes

To get to the summit of Mill Hill, there are two different trails to consider. The easiest is the **Auburn Trail** that leaves the parking lot at the far right. Only after a fork in the trail, where you should keep right, does the trail start to climb gradually to the summit with nice view points along the way. Some are better than at the 650-ft. summit.

A mildly more difficult trail is **Calypso Trail,** named after the abundance of Calypso orchids (Fairyslipper) between April and June. If it has been rainy, watch out for a slippery rock section. Going up is safer than heading down. If you would like a circular hike, I recommend you start with the more challenging **Calypso Trail**, enjoy the summit where there are breathtaking views overlooking Esquimalt Harbour and parts of Victoria, and then continue the gradually descending **Auburn Trail** just south of the summit, off the **Calypso Trail**.

You can make a longer, more adventurous hike, if you and your dog are up to it. The **Calypso Trail** continues northeast and descends into **Thetis Regional Lake Park**. It is only about one kilometer to the parks border, but one has to continue at the other side of the Trans Canada Highway.

85

Trail sense
Certain areas in Mill Hill Park are under a restoration program to improve the Garry Oak Ecosystem. Please stay on trails to support this cause.

Swimming Not available

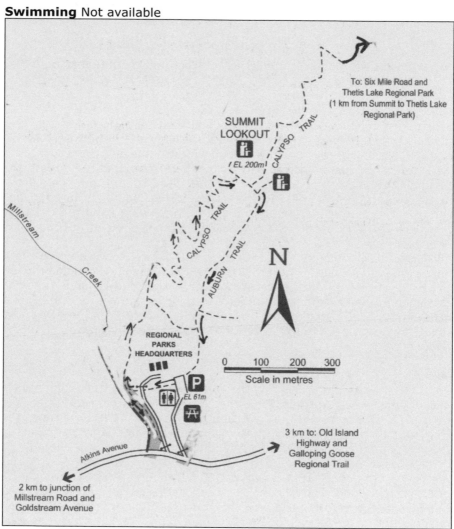

Map courtesy of CRD Parks

Directions to get there
From Victoria, follow the Trans-Canada Highway (# 1) and take the Colwood exit. Follow the Old Island Highway. Turn right on Six Mile Road, then left on Atkins Avenue. Turn left at the four-way stop to continue on Atkins Avenue, which leads to the park entrance on the right.

🚗 approximately 25 minutes from Victoria.

Locater Map, Nanaimo and Duncan Areas

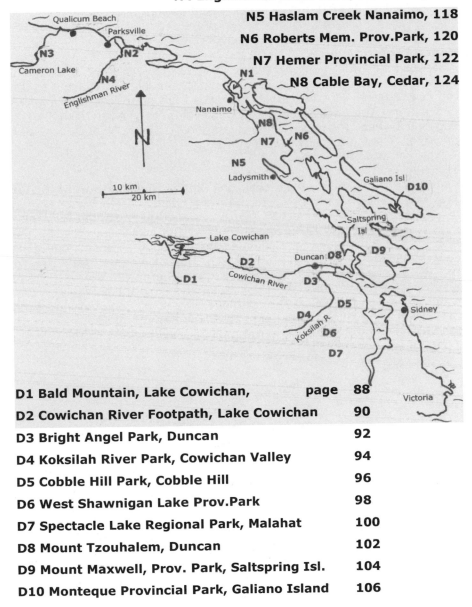

D 1   Bald Mountain, Cowichan Lake

Trail difficulty 🐾 🐾 🐾
Trail condition ☺ - ☹
Time/ length   5-6 hrs. loop
Admission   None
Parking   Free, but limited
Hours   dawn to dusk
Restrictions   Dogs should be controlled
Overall Rating   🦴🦴🦴🦴

General Information

A serious hike awaits you on a peninsula in Lake Cowichan. The terrain is variable and has plenty of challenging sections before you make it to the top of the bluffs. The elevation difference from start to finish is about 465 meters. This makes it a hardy hike for even the best-conditioned dog and owner. The rewards however, are stunning views over Lake Cowichan, Gordon and McKenzie Bay.

The Hike

Walk past the gate for just over one km to the **Denninger Scout Trailhead**, which branches off to the right. Soon you start your ascend in a counter-clockwise direction towards a saddle. From here is a nice view towards the north shore and Youbou. The trail leads west on the ridge to the 629m summit. Continue west for about one km. one goes down gradually until the trail turns south. Here begins the challenge. At the steepest section is a fixed cable to help you down. The best views are from the west bluffs and they make the descend a real joy. Just watch your steps! Down at the lake level is a small campground where the hike takes a left along the easy to follow **Beaver Walk.** This follows the lakeside all the way back to the trailhead and parking. Total distance is over 8 km.

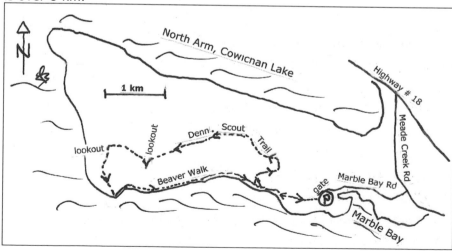

88

Trail sense

Make sure you are up to this hike. Some scrambling might be required during ascending or descending the steep bluffs on the south side of the mountain. There might be active logging in place so for that matter, the best day to do this hike would be a Sunday.

Swimming

Most parts along **Beaver Walk** are quite deep. Closer to the **Scouts Trailhead** there are some easy access spots for refreshing dips.

Bonus

Water and toilets are available at the trailhead.

Directions to get to the UVic Cowichan Lake Research Station Trailhead

Take theTrans-Canada highway (#1) to the Lake Cowichan highway (#18) just north of Duncan. Turn west (left) and drive 25.5 km taking the south fork to Lake Cowichan Village. At the Riverside Inn, turn right onto North Shore Road. Follow this to Meade Creek Road, turning left onto this road. Drive until you cross Meade Creek Bridge turning left again onto Marble Bay Road. Drive until you come to a gate at about 1.5 km where you can park

🚗 Total distance from Victoria is about 100 km.

D 2 Cowichan River Park, Skutz Falls, Cow. Valley

Trail difficulty 🐾 - 🐾🐾
Trail condition ☺
Time/ length 8 km loop
Admission None
Parking Free
Hours Dawn to Dusk
Restrictions Dogs should be on leash.
Overall Rating 🦴🦴🦴🦴

General information

Cowichan is from the Coast Salish word "Khowutzun." This means "land warmed by the sun," which causes the brisk daily winds on Cowichan Bay and Lake. It is an area rich in First Nations, mining and lumber history. The first European settlers to the region arrived in 1862. Agriculture dominated the early colonial years. Mining replaced agriculture as the primary industry when the interior opened up. However, forestry has the greatest impact on the valley. Most of the old-growth forest was logged in the early 1900s, and forestry activities continue to this day.

During your visit in the area, watch out for the many species of birds and wildlife. Small mammals found in the park include shrews, voles, bats and the native red squirrel. Raccoons, mink, martens and weasels are also common, and river otters and beavers inhabit the river. Larger mammals include black bears, which can be seen in the park during spawning, as well as cougars, black-tailed deer and Roosevelt elk.

The Hike

From the parking area, head down to the restored **66-Mile Trestle** and cross the river. The trestle is part of the famous **Trans Canada Trail** (see West Shawnigan Lake Park), and down river, look at the beautiful **Marie Canyon**. Our 8 km loop requires us to turn right after the trestle, following the southern riverside, west. This section is well marked with

kilometer markers. Spectacular views over the Cowichan River will come up at several points along this steep canyon area. At the midway point, 4 km, you will start to hear the rush of **Skutz Falls** and can cross the river over a truck bridge. Here is a good view of the falls. Past the bridge, look for the trail again on your right, and follow the river on the north side back to your parked car at **66-Mile Trestle**.

90

Trail sense
Stay away from overhanging cliffs and be careful on slippery rock sections. Be aware of the variety of wildlife you could run into here. Keep Fido close if you don't want him to turn into cougar bait
.

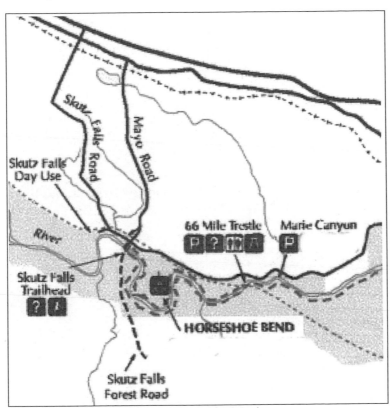

Map courtesy of BC Parks

Swimming
Severe rapids exist at Marike Canyon and Skutz Falls. Below the falls is swimming possible, but be aware of fluctuating water levels and swift currents.

How to get there
From Victoria, take the Trans-Canada Highway (#1) past Duncan. Turn left on Hwy # 18 and follow this west for about 17 km. Watch for the blue park sign and turn left onto Old Lake Cowichan Rd. Past the railway track, turn onto Stoltz Road. Turn right again on Riverbottom Road and drive for about 3 km to the **66-Mile Trestle** trailhead.

🚗 Take about one hour and twenty min. from Victoria or 20 min. from Duncan.

D 3   Bright Angel Park, Duncan

Trail difficulty 🐾
Trail condition ☺
Time/ length 1 hr
Admission   None
Parking   Free
Hours Dawn to Dusk
Restrictions   Dogs should be on leash
Overall Rating 🦴🦴🦴

General information

This is a small park, but has a lot to offer to most dog walkers. There is a maze of trails in the larger western section of the park. The big attraction however, is the suspension bridge and the fine gravel riverside you will reach at the eastern side.

The Walk

To stretch your walk to the maximum, find the trail leading around the perimeter of the western section. Once thre, you certainly must try the suspension bridge. Our Jazz gets a bit uneasy on a suspension bridge when it swings, too bad. Once at the other side, follow the river up-stream for about half a kilometer. You will pass by a rope-swing and find the trail that leads back to the bridge.

Trail sense

Do like the people in my picture, they keep Yombi on the leash, and clean up after. Yombi got a little too excited when I came close, and bit me almost in the arm.

Kristen with Yombi below the suspension bridge

Swimming

Great swimming here for both you and your dog. You'll find fine gravel along the river instead of sand.

How to get there

From Victoria take the Trans-Canada highway (#1) North over the Malahat. Turn left at the lights at Koksilah Road. (about 6 km before Duncan) Follow this road past the Koksilah River. At about half a kilometer past the bridge, you will get a park sign to turn right. Go slow into the park and park at the end.

Take about one hour from Victoria or 10 min from Duncan.

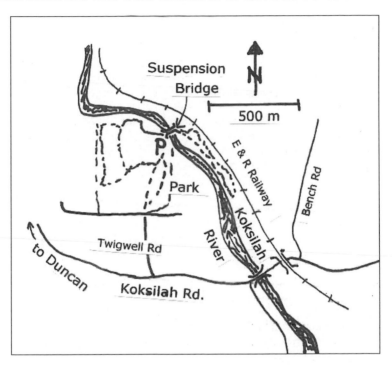

D 4   Koksilah River Park, Shawnigan Lake area

Trail difficulty 🐾 - 🐾 🐾
Trail condition ☺ ☻
Time/ length 4 km +
Admission   None
Parking   Free
Hours   dawn - dusk
Restrictions   Dogs should be on leash
Overall Rating 🦴🦴🦴🦴

General information

This is an undeveloped park in the Vancouver Island Forest Reserve that offers good hiking, fishing and swimming opportunities. The river can be wild depending on previous rainfall and runs through a canyon. Nearby, actually before you reach the park, there is an interesting section of the **Trans Canada Trail** that leads north to one of the world's largest wooden trestles. With other beautiful hikes such as **West Shawnigan Lake Park** (see D6) nearby, I recommend a weekend outing to this area. A good place to camp is at Clearwater Campsite.

The Hike

From the small parking area on the south side of Port Renfrew Road, cross the road and take the easy gravel topped **Trans Canada Trail** for about 2 km northwards. This will get you to the large historic **Kinsol Trestle**.
Unfortunately, this huge trestle is in bad repair and cannot be crossed pending restoration. Until funding for repair comes into place, two large viewing platforms, one on each side of the river, have been installed. There is an 8.5 km bypass to get to the other side if you like.
On your way back, head east from the trail and you can pick up the **Kaptara trails** leading to some fine viewpoints.

Another Hike is possible when driving to the bridge in Koksilah Provincial Park. Cross the bridge (closed to traffic at time of writing) and follow the river along the north side. This is not well marked and is moderate in difficulty. Another option is to follow the gravel road for less than 2 km and take the open trail over rock to a lookout point at the northwest.

Trail sense

These trails are quiet and Fido for that matter, might enjoy some freedom, but be aware that cougar and black bear sightings are not uncommon in the area.

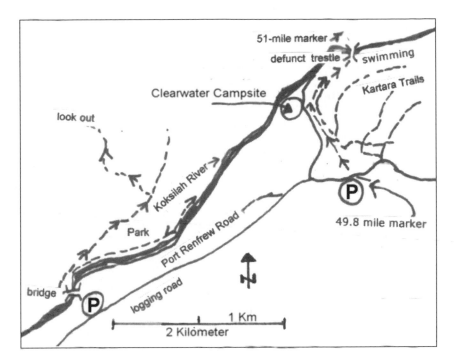

Swimming

The Koksilah River offers many nice spots for Bowser to have a swim,
however the easiest acces is right from the Clearwater Campsite where
your hosts are very dog-friendly.

How to get there

From Victoria take the Trans-Canada highway (#1) North over the
Malahat. Turn left at the lights past the village of Mill Bay and follow this
road for about 15 km to Shawnigan Lake. Continue along the northeast
shore on to Port Renfrew Road. Before 2 km, you will see a small parking
lot on the left trailhead or go for 7 km to Koksilah Park.
🚗 Take about one hour from Victoria or 20 min from Duncan.

Clearwater Campsite	44 full service sites
2970 Glen Eagle Rd.	1.5 acres riverfront
Shawnigan Lake	Dog Friendly, great
250 - 743 - 3569	hiking, swimming and
	Steelhead fishing

D 5   Cobble Hill and Quarry Park, Cobble Hill

Trail difficulty   🐾 - 🐾 🐾
Trail condition   ☺
Time/ length 5 km loop
Admission   None
Parking   Free
Hours   Dawn to Dusk
Restrictions   None
Overall Rating 🦴🦴🦴

General information

Here we have two parks adjacent to one another. The smaller Quarry Wilderness Park that has some easy gravel trails of its own and the larger Cobble Hill forest reserve.

The Quarry used to be a Lime quarry and was abandoned during the last century. From here, there is a good hike to the 1000 ft. summit of Cobble Hill. There are other access points, one of which is about 600 meters south on Empress Ave.

The Hike

From the parking lot, go past the pit-toilet and follow the gravel path west through Quarry Park. At an intersection, take a right. You are now in Cobble Hill Park. Veer left and you will slowly start ascending.

At the next trail on the right, a sign will indicate the trail to the summit. Actually there are three steep trails of which the center one is best for hiking. The others are for equestrian use.

At the summit, there are a few more worthwhile lookout points. One point is on the right and the best one is past the actual summit. If you are limited in time, take the same trail down and continue south to where the intersection was, before the steep ascend. After about half a kilometer, veer left for another kilometer where a sign indicates the straight trail back to Quarry Park.

Trail sense

Sharing trails with horses asks for common sense. Leave the wild flowers and be aware of wildlife.

Swimming

None

How to get there

From Victoria take the Trans-Canada Highway (#1) North over the Malahat. Turn left at the lights at Hutchinson Road, a few lights past the village of Mill Bay, and follow this road to the train tracks at Shawnigan Lake. Road. Cross the tracks and turn right into the parking lot at Quarry Park.

🚗 Take about 50 min. from Victoria or 20 min from Duncan.

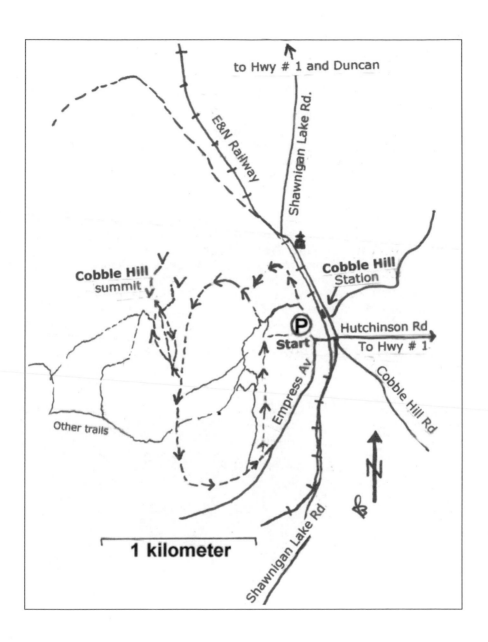

to Hwy # 1 and Duncan

E&N Railway

Shawnigan Lake Rd.

Cobble Hill
summit

Cobble Hill
Station

Other trails

P
Start

Hutchinson Rd
To Hwy # 1

Empress Av

Cobble Hill Rd

Shawnigan Lake Rd.

N

1 kilometer

D 6 West Shawnigan Lake Park, Shawnigan Lake

Trail difficulty 🐾
Trail condition ☺
Time/ length 9 km loop
Admission None
Parking Free
Hours 9 am – 9 pm
Restrictions Dogs should be on leash and are not allowed in the beach area from May 1 – Sept.15
Overall Rating 🐾🐾🐾

General information

This is a small park mainly used for swimming and picnicking in the summer. It is however a good start or finish point for a great hike along a part of the **Trans Canada Trail**. Actually, the part here is called the Cowichan Valley Trail, and makes use of the old Canadian North Pacific Railway bed. Originally from the early 1900s, CN took the railway over in 1913 to have it connect to Port Alberni. Due to other means in timber transport, the plans were abandoned. In 1979, use of this railway was discontinued and during the following decade, the railroad was removed. The empty rail-bed with its many historic trestles is now part of the **Trans Canada Trail**, which will stretch for about 16,000 km, from coast to coast. Once it is all finished, it will be the longest hiking trail in the world.

The Hike

The park has a short trail through a Douglas fir forest to the large open grassy play area and beach. Follow this south and by the park boundary, follow the road south for another few hundred meters to **McGee Creek Drive**. Take this road and on your right, a small parking area is right in front of the **Trans**

Canada Trail information kiosk. Now before you hike north on this easy to follow gravel trail, go south for a moment and have a look at the nicely renovated McGee Creek trestle.

The trail more or less parallels the road going north, though never too close to make it annoying. After one mile is a marker at Shawnigan Wye. From that point, it is only another 2.5 km before the trail meets up with the road. Here is a small parking area and one could head back by road or trail.

Trail sense

If you bring more than one car, it would make sense to drop a car off at one end. A bicycle could provide the same solution if you were with two or more people. In that case, I would do the trail the other way around. Leave the bicycle at the park near the beach and the car at the trailhead off Port Renfrew Road. That way Bowser can spend some time at the beach while one of you picks up the car.

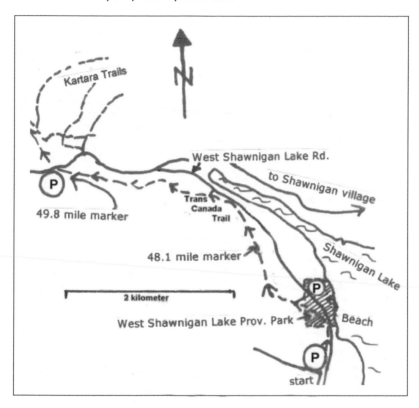

Swimming

From September 16 to April 30, all dogs can swim from the grassy south-east facing beach. The front gate of the park might be closed from October 31 to May 23, so you'll need to find alternate parking. Still, the hike to the beach should not be more than a few hundred meters.

How to get there

From Victoria, take the Trans-Canada Highway (#1) west, over the Malahat. Turn left at the lights past the village of Mill Bay and follow this road for about 15 km to the lake. Continue along the northeast shore and turn left at West Shawnigan Lake Road for a few kilometers to the park.

🚗 Take about one hour from Victoria or 20 min from Duncan.

D 7   Spectacle Lake Regional Park, Malahat

Trail difficulty 🐾 - 🐾 🐾
Trail condition ☺ ☹
Time/ length 2 km +
Admission   None
Parking   Free
Hours   dawn to dusk
Restrictions   Dogs should be leashed at all times and are not allowed on the beach.
Overall Rating 🦴🦴🦴

Park information

Mature forest and wetlands surround a spring-fed, freshwater lake. This is one of the few accessible lakes between Victoria and Nanaimo that allows swimming, fishing and even skating in winter. Due to its elevation, it is one of the first frozen bodies of water in the area each year.

Hikes

An easy 2 km well maintained trail circles the 'spectacles' shaped lake; hence its name. Wooden bridges and a boardwalk cross the numerous creeks and marshy areas and keep this trail easy to finish in under an hour.

To extend your hike, consider **Oliphant Lake** as your destination.

From the northeast end of Spectacle Lake, a good trail branches northwards and ascends gradually. After about 30 minutes (2 km), you come to a T-junction on a ridge. Take a left, which drops down and joins a truck road that circles **Oliphant Lake**. Completing this hike, will take you 3 to 4 hours, depending on your speed. Or is the dog holding you back?

Trail sense

Be careful on the boardwalk, it can be very slippery under wet conditions. Don't shortcut trails; it destroys plants and soil structure.

If you continue on to **Oliphant Lake**, expect to get your feet wet. Some sections are prone to flooding.

Swimming

Dogs are not allowed on the beach, but that should not deter you or Max from swimming in this fresh-water lake. There are other access points to get in the lake for that refreshing dip. Pooch will love it here.

Bonus

A water pump is found at the picnic area. If you have a permit, fish for Cutthroat trout or better yet; your only chance on Vancouver Island to catch Eastern Brook trout.

100

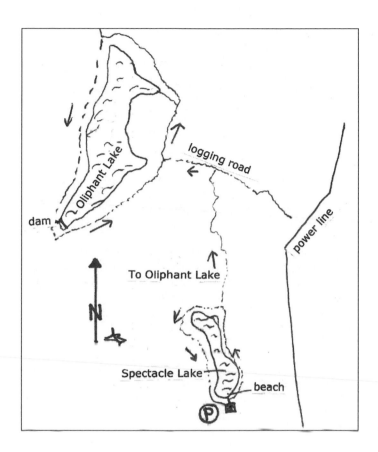

Directions to get there

Take highway #1(the Trans-Canada) west from Victoria. Shortly past the first Shawnigan Lake cut-off at the 'Aerie' hotel sign, turn left on Whitaker Road. Follow this road by going left at the first junction. At about one km from here, look for a gravel road on your right, this will take you to the Spectacle Lake parking area.

🚗 Take about 35 minutes from Victoria.
From the northwest, watch for the blue Spectacle Lake park sign just past the summit on the Malahat drive. Turn right on Whitaker Road.

D 8   Mount Tzouhalem, North Cowichan, Maple Bay

Trail difficulty 🐾 🐾 🐾
Trail condition 😊
Time/length 7 km one way
Admission   None
Parking   Free
Hours Dawn to Dusk
Restrictions Little restrictions, but on leash in the Ecological Reserve.
Overall Rating 🦴🦴🦴🦴

General information
This mountain really stands out as a challenging landmark to be conquered. There are three good hikes up to the 536-meter summit. The closest to Duncan offers some cheating options by car, if you find about 1,630 some-odd feet too much to climb.

Some strange history is responsible for the mountain's name change from Cowichan Mountain to Mount Tzouhalem. During the first part of the 1800s, a member of the Cowichan Tribe by the name Tzouhalem lived in a cave on the mountain. He had a stroke of bad luck, being born with an abnormality. Losing his mother and younger brother in a fight with the Haida, he turned violent. G.P.V. Akrigg, in *1001 British Colombia Place Names*, writes: "Because of his frequent murders he was banished at last by his tribe, and took up residence in a cave on the side of Mount Tzuhalem. With him he had some 14 wives, most of whom had been widowed by him." The story goes on and on and does not get any prettier.
Nowadays, the mountain is quite safe to visit and a huge white iron cross on the west side used to be a pilgrimage destination by the Sisters of Saint Ann on Good Friday.

The Hike
From **Genoa Bay**, many boaters try this tough hike, and so did we years ago when Jazz was still young and strong.
From the Marina parking lot, simply walk back a bit along the road to the first sideroad and find the trailhead by walking past the fence. It is a long, steady climb with some steep sections here and there.
Eventually you will come to the main logging road that leads to the summit. This one way will take you about two hours. If you are still up for some more, another half hour will bring you to the cross, from where there are magnificent views west. The trail left from the summit going west, used to be marked yellow and blue. Stay on the upper trail until you come to a T-junction, where you go right. Now on a logging road veer left at the junction. After a while, the road ends up as a trail and runs down through a gully. Left again will bring you to the south bluff, where the trail goes westward to the cross.
Leave enough time for your return.

102

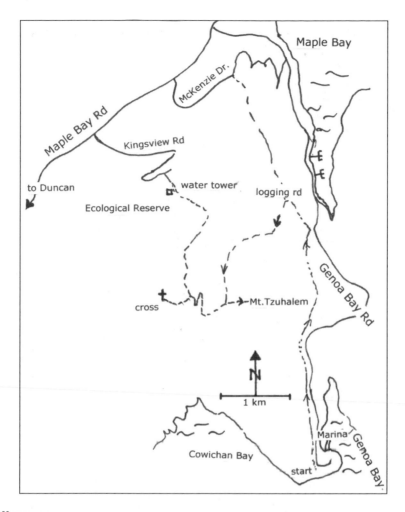

Trail sense
Bring enough water for this somewhat strenuous hike.

Swimming
After you make it back, Rover would love to cool down in the water at the marina. Go to the end of the docks. The water there is a lot cleaner than at the beach.

How to get there
From Victoria take the Trans-Canada highway (#1) to Duncan. Turn right at Trunk Rd.; (past the bridge) follow the signs to Maple Bay. Just before Maple Bay, Genoa Bay Road will come up, which you follow to the end of the road where you can find parking.

🚗 About one an a half hours from Victoria or 30 min from Duncan.

D 9 Mount Maxwell, Provincial Park, Saltspring Island

Trail difficulty 🐾 🐾
Trail condition ☺
Time/ length 1.5 hrs
Admission None
Parking free
Hours sunrise to sunset
Restrictions Keep dogs leashed at all times
Overall Rating 🦴🦴🦴🦴

Park information
Since this park requires a short ferry ride, one would need the better part of a day to do it. Why not combining this hike with a visit to the art and farmers market on Saturday morning held in Ganges.

Mt. Maxwell was originally established for its distinctive landmark viewing point in 1938. The 197-hectare mountaintop park was expanded to nearly 1,000 hectares in 2001 to conserve Burgoyne Bay. The park now stretches from mountaintop to shoreline and across **Burgoyne Bay** to the slopes of Mount Bruce. This park contains the highest point, 594 meters, on Saltspring Island with some spectacular panoramic views over Burgoyne Bay, Sansum Narrows and Maple Bay.

Mount Maxwell is an important place in the Cowichan First Nation traditions. Known as Hwmat'etsum, or "bent over place," it features in origin stories about the relationship of man and the land. Archaeological sites of spiritual significance lie below the adjacent Mount Maxwell Ecological Reserve.

Ganges market

Hikes
From the first parking areas, just along the road when you enter the park boundary, take a route south through open forest towards the cliffside trail. After about 400 meters, pick up the cliffside trail turning left where you soon will get the first of three lookout points.

At about 2 km from the start, you will reach the top of **Baynes Peak**, where the most spectacular viewpoint is located. Be careful with keeping Bowser on your side of the fence. The drop-off is steep and dangerous here, but gives you a unique opportunity to see the topside of soaring raptors such as eagles, turkey vultures or Peregrine falcons. If it's foggy, the floating mist also has its charm, but intend to come back on a clear day to enjoy the sunset and marvel at the panoramic views.

From the peak, a trail goes in a southeasterly direction through old growth and eventually turns to the left. At an intersection, take the left trail which will gradually take you back (two more lefts) to the larger parking area and road where you will find your car.
Total distances approximate 6-7 km.

Trail sense
There are some threatened rare plant species in the park. Staying on trails will help protect them. Stay well behind the fenced cliff-side area unless you plan to skydive with your pet.

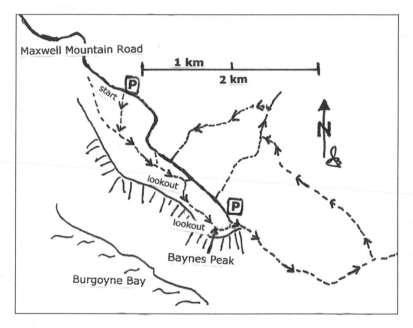

Swimming None available in this park.

Directions to get there
Take BC Ferries to Saltspring Island from Victoria (Swartz Bay) or Crofton on Vancouver Island. From Fulford, Saltspring Island, take the road to Ganges and at about 2 km before you reach the town, look for Cranberry Road on the left. Follow this to a junction with Mount Maxwell Road take a left again. Continue slowly on the rough road to the park. This gravel road is steep, narrow and bumpy; be careful.

🚗 approximately 1.5 hours (including ferry) from Victoria.

D 10 Montague Harbour, Provincial Park, Galiano Island

Trail difficulty 🐾 🐾
Trail condition ☺
Time/ length   1 hr +
Admission   None
Parking $ 1.00 -$ 3.00
Hours sunrise to sunset
Restrictions Keep dogs leashed at all times
Overall Rating 🦴🦴🦴🦴🦴

Park information

This is actually a Marine Park and is located on peaceful Galiano Island. There is a rich natural and cultural history with white shell beaches, open meadows, a tidal lagoon, and a beautiful circular hike around it all. Since this is a marine park, the boundary starts five meters below sea level and climbs 180 meters to a steep rocky precipice.

Hiking here however, is fairly level and the prettiest part is around the **Gray Peninsula**, This place was inhabited by First Nations peoples before the arrival of Spanish explorer Dionisio Galiano in 1792. Archaeological excavations of protected middens have unearthed arrows, spearheads and primitive stone carvings, helping to unravel the stories of earlier cultures.

Hike

A hike in the park is limited to about 4 km. and if that is all you plan to do, park in the park (fee $ 3.). Take a right at the end of the parking lot and sweep left. This path is on the campground and will soon reach the boa tramp and the stairs to the real trail that follows the shore for almost the entire balance of this hike. On a sunny day, the white shell beach on the north side of the park is spectacular, but blinding to the eye. It is one of several shell middens – evidence of native occupation dating back more than 3,000 years. Wave action erodes the middens, crushes the shells and re-deposits them to create Montague's white shell beaches.

Next, the hike skirts the northwest edge of the **Gray Peninsula** where the spectacular rock ledge is carved into rippling patterns by the movement of glaciers thousands of years ago. Turning south, one has more white beaches that invite your dog running or swimming. At the southeast end, you will see the boats in the harbour again and hiking north, keep an eye out for the shallow sections to cross the lagoon if possible. At high tide, keep the lagoon to the right and follow it clockwise around to the other end where you cross the campground back to the parking area. Note the water pump, just when you come up from the lagoon into the campground. A welcoming gesture after one or two hours hiking.

Another option is, when you come by car from the **Sturdies Bay** ferry, to park 2 km before the park near the old ferry dock-ramp, just past the marina. From here, follow the quiet asphalt road to the park with occasional nice views into **Montague Harbour**. Nowadays there will be boats anchored year-round, that make a nice backdrop in this serene environment. In the park, follow the road all the way north to the boat launch and follow directions from above. This will make a nice two-hour hike.

Trail sense
Keep Fido on the leash and don't shortcut the trails to protect the forest. The rocky coastline and tidal lagoon attract many birds year-round such as Great Blue Herons, Glaucous-winged gulls, Black oystercatchers, Northwestern crows, Belted kingfisher and Bald eagles.

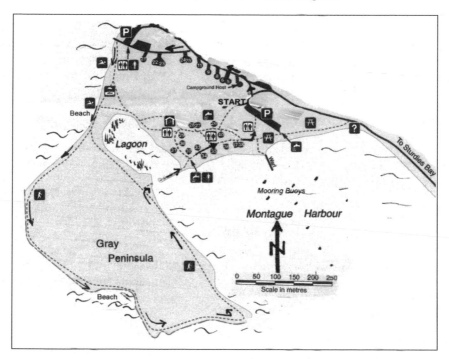

Swimming
This park has one of the nicest beaches described In this guide, what a great place for a swim. Not at the main beach for dogs, but it is easy to find other suitable sections to wet the appetite.
Bonus Horse clams, littleneck clams and butter clams can be found beneath the shifting sands off the shore.

Directions to get there
Montague Harbour Park is located on the west side of Galiano Island approximately 10 km northwest of Sturdies Bay where the BC Ferry comes in from Swartz Bay on Vancouver Island and from Tsawwassen, from the mainland. The park is located on Montague Park Road; follow signs to the park from the ferry terminal
🚗 45 minutes + ferry from Swartz Bay.

N 1   New Castle Island, Provincial Park, Nanaimo

Trail difficulty   🐾

Trail condition   ☺

Time/ length 1- 3 hrs

Admission see foot passenger ferry info below

Parking fee   Yes

Hours see ferry schedule

Restrictions Dogs should be leashed.

Overall Rating 🦴🦴🦴🦴🦴

General Information

On my first visit, years ago, the stunning beauty of this island immediately struck me. It was on a marine biology study-trip early in the year. Cold as it was, we made a lunch stop at neighboring **Protection Island** to warm up at the cozy Dinghy Dock Pub, which claims to be the only 'floating pub' in Canada. Since then I have been back almost a hundred times and I am always surprised again with the feel of remoteness and tranquility on these islands, while so close to downtown Nanaimo.

This 300 acres island is actually a Marine Park and thus only accessible by boat. Plenty of pleasure craft anchor in the basin near the island and make use of the docks to land on Newcastle Island. It is not always easy to get an eighty-pound dog in and out of a dinghy. Our Jazz always refuses to jump. It's much easier to take the regular foot passenger ferry.

The ferry runs from May 1 to Thanksgiving, and will be happy to take you and Woofus for the 10-minute ride.

There is an extensive network of trails, well marked and, except for a few rises here and there, very easy to hike. You can walk from a moderate two kilometers to an extended 8 km. hike, which takes you around the beautiful perimeter of the entire island.

A lot of History

In the early days, huge coal deposits were found below the island and further out below the bottom of the ocean. I guess that if it were Scotchmen that came in the mid 1800s, the island would have been called Glasgow Island. But it were British immigrants that sailed by the boatloads and came to work in the coalmines and so, they named it after their famous English coal town.

Before the coal was discovered, Salish First Nations used to live on two sections of the island during the winter months.

Industry has tried many different things since. After the coal was depleted in 1883, sandstone was quarried and used in numerous important buildings along the west coast from here to San Francisco. In 1910, the Japanese, who dominated fisheries at that time, had a small settlement just north of Shaft Point on the west side of the Island. They operated a saltery and shipyard until Japan became involved in World War 2. On the other side of the Island, the Canadian Pacific Steamship

Company operated a resort after they bought the Island in 1931. You can still see what was once the dance pavilion, is now the visitor's center and concession area, just up from the landing dock. At that time, old cruise-liners were tied to the dock, utilizing them as floating hotels. Imagine, at one time they brought in as many as 1,500 people. The fun was short lived with the Second World War looming.

There have been two owners since, the City of Nanaimo and now, the Province of BC.

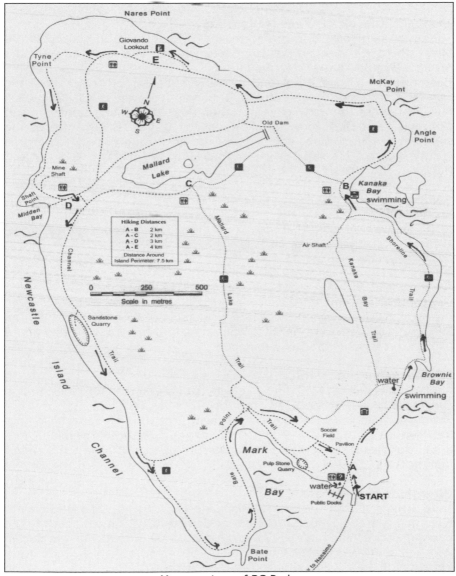

Map courtesy of BC Parks

Hikes
Several hikes are possible. Depending on the weather, you might decide to access some more protected interior hikes, or go for the full circle. We like to follow the entire shoreline, which has at certain points dramatic sandstone cliffs and ledges mixed in with beaches, rocky caves, and caverns. Walk straight north off the boat ramp. Watch out for all the geese droppings in the first section. Soon, you will pass the campground and hit the shore at **Brownie Bay**. Follow the **Shoreline Trail** and keep right to **Kanaka Bay**, where the best swimming area is. This is the quarter marker if you do the full circle. You have the option here for a short cut to the old dam and **Mallard Lake**.

The nicest viewpoint is at the north shore. Keep right and go up to the bluff, where **Giovando Lookout** gives you marvelous views over the Strait of Georgia to the Coast Mountains.

Continue on to **Tyne Point** and follow the shore southward where the Japanese settlement once stood. A short side trail brings you to a mineshaft from the early days. Another short connection brings you to **Channel Trail that** you can follow, all the way to **Bate Point** at the southern tip. From here, you can see the docks and hope your ferry is waiting for you. It's still 1.5 km around Mark Bay from here, so time it right.

Swimming
Kanaka Bay is definitely the best area, but you might see other spots along the way. An area that warms up nicely is between the main picnic area and Protection Island, up to Brownie Bay.

Bonus
Good drinking water is available at different points on the island. During the summer months, on Wednesday evening, it is a lot of fun to watch the local sailclub's race in the basin or outside of Protection Island. The best place to watch the finish is while having a burger with fries and a pint on the decks of the Floating Pub.

Footpassenger ferry info.
Adult tickets are $ 7.00 for a return trip. Discounts for Seniors and children. Children under 3 and dogs travel free.

From the beginning of May to Thanksgiving, the ferry leaves on the hour between 10 am and 5 or 6 pm. On Friday and Saturday evening there are extra departures with the last departure at 9 pm during the summer months. Call 250-754-7893 to confirm.

Directions to get there
Take Hwy # 1 from Victoria to Nanaimo. Follow the old highway into town and past the center. Turn right at Comox Road and direct left to the parking area behind the Civic Arena. A short walk through Maffeo Sutton Park will get you to the ferry dock.

🚐 approximately 2 hours (including ferry) from Victoria.

The beach at Roberts Memorial Provincial Park on a busy, hot July Saturday afternoon

N 2   **Rathtrevor Beach**, Provincial Park, Parksville

Trail difficulty	🐾
Trail condition	☺
Time/ length	4 km
Admission	None
Parking	$ 1. -$ 5.00
Hours	Dawn to Dusk
Restrictions	Dogs should be leashed at all times.
Overall Rating	🦴🦴🦴🦴

General information

The park offers only about 5 km of easy walking trails, but one can extend this by following the shoreline south. Depending on the tide, this can become heavy hiking through deep loose sand or nice going, over hard, wet sand.

Rathtrevor is named after an Irish family who homesteaded on this land. William Rath, a gold prospector, arrived in 1886 with his young wife and baby daughter. The land was cleared and they built a log cabin and a barn. The old Irishman died in 1903, leaving his wife the farm and five children. She was entrepreneurial, running the farm and eventually operating it successfully as a campground. The suffix 'trevor' was added to give the campground a more lyrical name. Rathtrevor Campground became Rathtrevor Beach Provincial Park in 1967.

The Walk

A very nice trail meanders along the beach. To get the most out of it, go from the first parking lot left past the park office through the campground, following the right boundary. Between spot # 21 and 22, take the trail that leads to the park boundary and turns toward the shore. From here, it is pure pleasure, soaking in the scents of the ocean and marvelous views across the Strait of Georgia. Towards the point, the trail branches off here and there, but as long as you keep following the left options, you will come around the point to where the best views are.

At low tide, the flats get large numbers of foraging birds. During spring, when thousands of Brant Geese feed here, dogs are off-limits. At that time, take an inland trail that runs from the end of the parking lots through mature forests of Douglas fir, Western red cedar, hemlock, balsam and spruce trees, towards the southern boundary. From there you can follow the high tide line past private properties and resorts until you get tired and want to turn around. In the park, this walk amounts to about 3 km and depending of what you do south of the park, this can turn out into a good size hike if you like.

On cold or windy days, there is the option for a short, protected walk around the old heritage farm field. Detailed trail maps are posted at information shelters in the park.

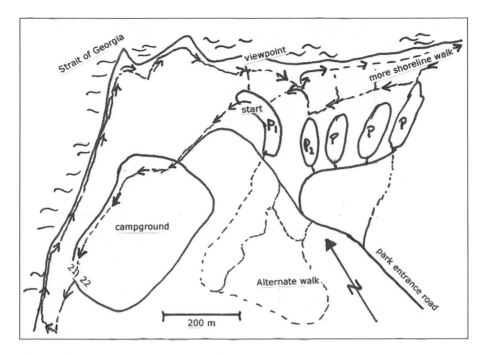

Swimming
Too shallow for yourself, most of the time, but for our dogs, splashing and running will be a blast. There are restrictions from March 15th to October 15th in the day-use area, but the west shore is fine. Please obey the signs.

Bonus
Many water faucets throughout the park will make 'Prince' never run thirsty for long, except during winter, when they are shut off.

How to get there
From Victoria take the Trans-Canada highway (#1) to Nanaimo where you go around and take Hwy #19 to Parksville. The park is actually 3 km south of Parksville on Hwy 19a. Take exit # 51 from the Inland Island Highway (Hwy #19) and follow signs to the park.

🚗 About two hours from Victoria or 30 min. from Nanaimo.

N 3   Little Qualicum Falls. Provincial Park, Qualicum

Trail difficulty   🐾
Trail condition   ☺
Time/ length 4 km loop
Admission None
Parking $ 1.00 -$ 3.00
Hours   Dawn to Dusk
Restrictions Dogs should be on a leash
Overall Rating 🦴🦴🦴🦴

General information
This park was established in 1940 to protect the old growth Douglas-fir forest. The park now also incorporates the picturesque southern shore of Cameron Lake nearby. Steep mountain peaks surround this truly forested area. The falls are impressive, particularly after a good rainfall.

The Hike
Walk from the parking area past the picnic shelter to the river. Turn left and follow the trail upstream. Soon you will hear the thundering sounds of the **Upper Falls** cascading down. Cross the bridge and turn left following the river for about one and a half km on the west side. Note the old-growth interchanging with the second-growth forest around you. Another bridge brings you back to the east side and on to the Lower Campground. Stay close to the river and where a bend in the river appears, you'll find a nice swimming area. The trail follows the river very closely all the way to the next bend. Now you'll be back at the **Upper Falls Bridge**. Cross it again and turn right to the little loop in the next bend. At the trail, go north to find the **Lower Falls**. Depending on your time, you can follow the river further downstream, but you'll have to come back to cross the **Lower Falls Bridge** again to get to your car.

Swimming
On the east side of the river, between the Upper and Lower Campground, swimming is alowed. Check the park information shelters for updates. **Lake Cameron** has a beautiful sandy shore and is only about 4 km farther along Hwy #4.

How to get there
From Victoria take the Trans-Canada highway (#1) to Nanaimo where you will go around and take Hwy #19 to Parksville. Turn off on Hwy #4 going west to Coombs. Look for the blue park signs and turn into the park where the larger parking lot is at the end. (19 km from Parksville).
🚗 Take about two hours from Victoria or 30 min from Nanaimo.

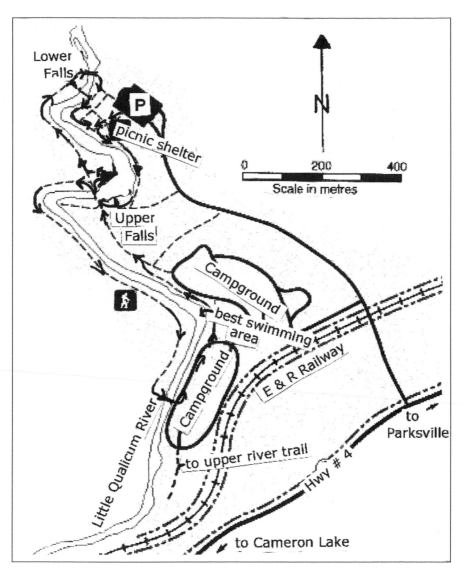

Little Qualicum Falls Provincial Park

#N 4 Englishman River Falls. Provincial Park, Parksville

Trail difficulty 🐾
Trail condition ☺
Time/ length 3 km loop
Admission None
Parking $ 1.00 -$ 3.00
Hours Dawn to Dusk
Restrictions Dogs should be on leash.
Overall Rating 🦴🦴🦴🦴

General information
About 13 km southwest of Parksville is a sharp bend in the pristine Englishman River. Surrounded by a mixed forest of evergreens and Arbutus are two waterfalls rushing through a narrow canyon. These were reasons enough to preserve the area and turn it into a popular Provincial Park. It is relative small, but one can turn this destination into a real hike by departing from the Top Bridge and follow the new created 5 km (one way) hike to **Rathtrevor Beach** (see there). Alternatively, just combine both parks by car.

The Walk
From the parking area, go beyond the information kiosk south toward the **Upper Falls**. This section is very picturesque, overlooking the falls from above. Watch your steps down to the bridge and cross to the other side where you could make a side trip by going right to a good viewpoint, or go left and continue down-river to the **Lower Falls**. Below the bridge is a good swimming hole. In autumn, this is a good spot to watch the salmon spawning.
Across the river, the trail first follows the riverbed for a while before turning back towards the picnic area and some more scenic sections of the trail towards the **Upper Bridge**. From here, take the path back to the parking area. Just the loop alone can be done in 30 minutes, but take the time to go up river along the south side if you have more time.

Trail Sense
If we like to keep these parks open to our canine friends, obey the regulations and pick up after your pet.

Swimming
Below the Lower Falls is a deep, crystal clear pool that offers comfort on a hot summer's day. Unfortunatly at time of writing, regulations prohibit dogs from dipping in at this spot. Perhaps a spot further down river is more suitable.

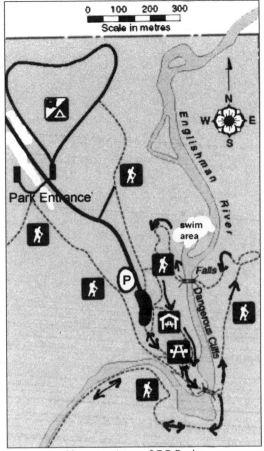

Map courtesy of BC Parks

How to get there

From Victoria, take the Trans-Canada Highway (#1) to Nanaimo where you take Hwy #18 north. Turn off on Hwy #4 going west and take Errington Road. Look for the blue park signs.

🚗 Take about two hours from Victoria or 30 min from Nanaimo.

N 5 Haslam Creek Suspension Bridge Trail, Nanaimo

Trail difficulty   🐾
Trail condition   ☺
Time/ length 1–3 hrs.
Admission   None
Parking fee optional
Hours   Dawn to Dusk
Restrictions None
Overall Rating 🦴🦴🦴🦴

General information
A recently completed part of the **Trans Canada Trail** has opened up thanks to cooperation between the Regional District of Nanaimo, the Provincial Government and the Trans Canada Trail Foundation. The highlight of this section is unmistakably the long, 48-meter (150 feet) suspension bridge over the **Haslam Creek**.
Locally the bridge is known fondly as 'Mindy's Bridge' in memory of Rene Bertrand's dog. She accompanied Rene and the volunteer trail team faithfully on countless forays into the bush. It was Mindy who actually found the beautiful spot along the creek where the bridge was to be built.

The Hike
There are two options here. The shorter is a 3 km circular hike that goes to the suspension bridge and back. Alternatively, the longer, 6 km one-way hike is to the next trailhead, a road access point (**Spruston Rd, McKay Lake**) where you could drop a car off in advance of your hike.
Either way, you could start from **Rondalyn Resort's** user pay parking area or find a safe spot along Timberlands Rd toward the gate's trailhead. Pass the gate and follow the logging road turning right. Past the wooden log-bridge, the trail turns left passing a small gravel pit. Watch for orange markers and tape. Do not take any of the three roads that branch off to the right. After the third road to the right, look to the left for the trail to the bridge.
For the circular hike, continue on straight, after you have gotten dizzy enough swinging 40 feet above the creek. By a car-wreck on the right, you should turn left, following the tree line. Most of the way you have a large gravel pit on the right until you descend to the logging road and

gate at the end of Timberlands Rd.

For the longer one-way trail, after you cross the bridge, follow the creek to the left. Keep following the trail markers. After about a mile, the trail leaves the creek side and the small **Timberlands Lake** will come up on the left. At this point, it is only a few more kilometers along the trail to **McKay Lake** and the **Spruston Rd** access point.

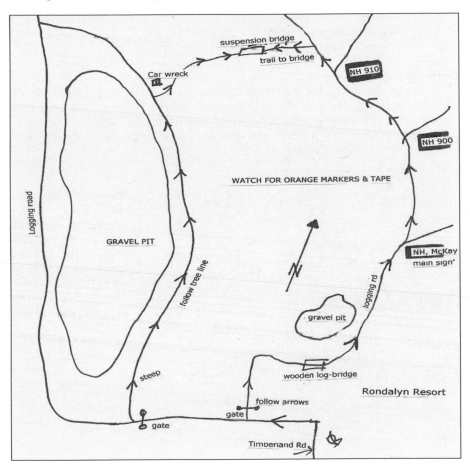

Swimming

Up from the bridge, along the wide bend in the creek is some wonderful splashing possible for dogs off all sizes.

How to get there

From Victoria, take the Trans-Canada Highway (#1) west, past Duncan and Ladysmith. Shortly past Ladysmith, at a traffic sign before the Nanaimo Airport, take Timberlands Rd on the left and follow it to the end.

🚗 Take about 90 minutes from Victoria or 15 min from Nanaimo.

N 6 Roberts Memorial Provincial Park, Yellow Point

Trail difficulty 🐾
Trail condition ☺
Time/ length 2 km return
Admission None
Parking Free
Hours Dawn to Dusk
Restrictions Dogs should be leashed
Overall Rating 🦴🦴🦴🦴

General information

This is a small park, not much for hiking, but has a really quiet beach with a wonderful view over Stuart Channel. When we were here on a hot, sunny Saturday afternoon in July, we were the only visitors in the park. Therefore, if you are looking for a short walk with easy access to a desolate beach, this is your park.

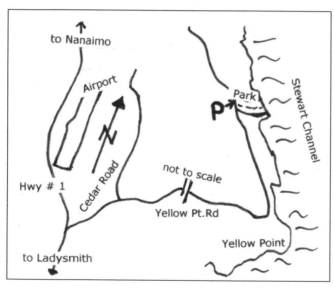

The Walk

An easy one-kilometer trail leads through secondary, mixed forest to the rocky, sandstone beach. With a bit of luck you might find some seals or sea lions that like to haul-out on the sandstone ledges.

Swimming

This would be the main reason for visiting this park. So, have fun.

How to get there

From Victoria take the Trans-Canada highway (#1) west towards Nanaimo. Take the Cedar Road turnoff south of Nanaimo. After a few minutes, take Yellow Point Rd on the right and follow that to the park, which is past the bend on the right.

From Nanaimo, take the first exit to Cedar. Follow Cedar Rd. south and turn off to Yellow Point Rd., on the left.

🚗 About 100 minutes from Victoria or 25 min. from Nanaimo.

The beach at Roberts Memorial Provincial Park on a 'busy,' hot July
Saturday afternoon

N 7   Hemer Provincial Park, Nanaimo,

Trail difficulty   🐾
Trail condition   ☺
Time/ length 4-6 km loop
Admission   None
Parking   Free
Hours Dawn to Dusk
Restrictions Dogs should be leashed.
Overall Rating 🦴🦴🦴🦴

General information
Getting here through a relatively new neighborhood, I was surprised to see the sudden pastoral setting at the parks entrance. From the site of the plaque commemorating the land-gift from John and Violet Hemer, one has a nice view over the large marshy area and the old farmstead.
Most trails are wide and easy, thanks to utilizing the abandoned Pacific Coal Company railway bed. This railway went to **Boat Harbour**, and one can extend the hike outside the park to continue onto the little boat basin.

The Hike
We took the **Heritage Trail**, and once past the pit-toilets, turned left down to **Holden Lake**. Following the shore for almost 2 km, the trail veers right to the park boundary. To **Boat Harbour** from here is still quite a distance, so we finished a loop by taking the trail across the creek and along the marsh back to the parking area. There is a large viewing platform by the marsh that makes it easy to spot the various types of ducks, Turkey vultures, Bald eagles and Trumpeter Swans.
It took us almost two hours to go around, but our golden retriever Jazz, was almost thirteen then. She certainly takes her time now.

Pastoral setting at the park's entrance

Swimming
It will be hard to resist the easy access in **Holden Lake.**

How to get there
From Victoria take the Trans-Canada highway (#1) west towards Nanaimo. Take the Cedar Road turnoff south of Nanaimo and follow that for about 15 minutes. Just past the intersection with Yellow Point Rd, take Hemer Rd on the right. A small parking lot is at the park entrance at the end of the road.

🚙 Take about 100 minutes from Victoria or 20 min from Nanaimo

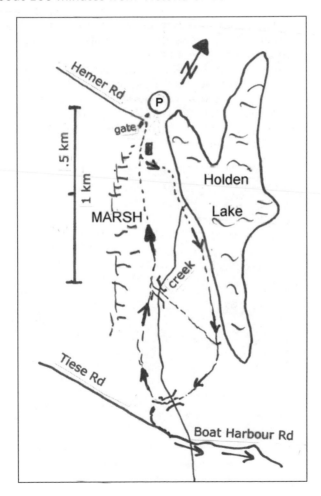

N 8   Cable Bay Trail, Nanaimo Regional District, Cedar

Trail difficulty   🐾
Trail condition   ☺
Time/ length 4 km plus
Admission None
Parking   Free
Hours   closed at 11 pm
Restrictions There are two designated off-leash sections
Overall Rating 🦴🦴🦴🦴

General information
Close to the Harmac Pulp Mill was the so-called Harmac Nature trail, which used a lot of private land. The District of Nanaimo has stepped in and has since relocated this trail to its current location and made it a permanent arrangement. Two specific side trails are designated for off-leash running, which is a great initiative.

At the bay, during fall and spring migration, one can watch many Californian sea lions on the floating logs near the shore. From here, the hike can be extended to **Dodds Narrows**. This is an interesting spot to watch boats sail through. Most boats queue up around slack (turnaround time of the tide) and once they go through the Narrows, it can be quite a busy spectacle to watch from shore.

The Hike
The well-maintained trail leaves the parking lot and veers left for a while. Within half a km, the first off-leash section branches off to the left. This trail is dead-end, so be sure to trace it back to where you originated. The main trail now veers right, and at the next bend to the left, the second off-leash section comes up on the right. Only the main trail of about 2 km leads to **Cable Bay**, which is a great spot for watching seabirds, sea lions in the fall and spring and Bald eagles during winter.

To the right, following the shore of the Northumberland Channel, it's about another km to **Joan Point** at **Dodds Narrows**. This section is not on public land, so be courteous to owners.

124

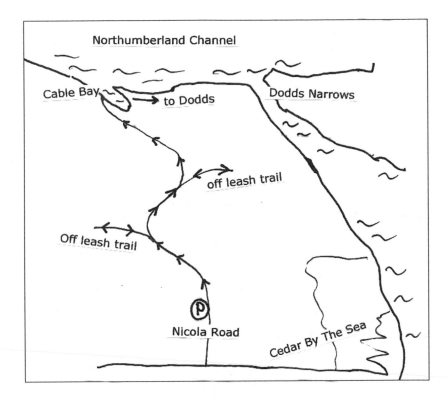

Northumberland Channel

Cable Bay → to Dodds

Dodds Narrows

off leash trail

Off leash trail

Ⓟ

Nicola Road

Cedar By The Sea

Swimming
The Bay has easy water access, so make it a happy day for Max.

How to get there
From Victoria, take the Trans-Canada Highway (#1) west towards Nanaimo. Take the turnoff to Cedar, just south of Nanaimo. In the village of Cedar, turn at the gas station onto Holdon Corso Rd and follow that for a few km. Past some sharp curves, watch for Nicola Rd on the left. Take that to the end and park.

🚗 Take about 100 minutes from Victoria or 20 min from Nanaimo.

Useful Web Addresses and Phone

Public Parks
B.C. Provincial Parks website   www.gov.bc.ca/bcparks
Capital Regional District Parks, www.crd.bc.ca/parks   (250) 478-3344
City of Victoria Parks,   www.city.victoria.bc.ca   (250) 361-0600
Cowichan Valley Rec.District, www.cvrd.bc.ca/parks   (250) 746-2500
Recreation Oak Bay,   www.district.oak-bay.bc.ca   (250) 595-7946
Regional District of Nanaimo, www.rdn.bc.ca/parks_rec/parks   1-888-828-2069
Saanich Parks,   www.gov.saanich.bc.ca   (250) 744-5341

Pet Care Services
S.P.C.A. Victoria 388-7722 SPCA Duncan: 746-4646, SPCA Nanaimo: 758-8444
Club Dog, Doggy Daycare at Gorge and Juttland   (250) 480-0234
Dog Company, Island Dog Sports. Training/ teaching services   (250) 656-1659
Kit'n Kapoodle, Pet Grooming, 597 Baxter Ave., Victoria   (250) 370-7807
Vagabond Pets Ltd. 24/7 loss protection service   (250) 213-6155
Happy Hound, Dogcare Company, 4408 Boban Dr. Nanaimo   (250) 756-0340

Pet Supplies Stores
A Pet's Life, at Fort & Foul Bay Ave., Victoria,   (250) 592-3301
Bosley's Pet Food Plus neighbourhood pet stores look for locations on page 128
Chez Terry's 1516 Fairfield Rd. 592-6911   and 3838 Cadboro Bay Rd 382-5299
Chow Barn Pet supplies, 1803 Fort Street Victoria   (250) 592-9954
Pets West, 777 Royal Oak dr., Victoria   (250) 744-1779
Ruff Creations, 2029 Oak Bay Ave.,Victoria,   (250) 592-9911
Woofles, a doggy diner and specialty store at Market Square   1-866-471-9663
Mill Bay Pets Plus, 2720 Mill Bay rd.,   Mill Bay,   (250) 743-3815

Veterinary Hospitals / Clinics
Cadboro Bay Veterinary Clinic, 2561 Sinclair Rd., Victoria,   (250) 477-9061
Central Victoria Veterinary Hospital, 760 Roderick St. Victoria,   (250) 475-2495
Oak Bay Pet Clinic, 1826 Oak Bay Ave., Victoria,   (250) 475-2495
Shaw Pet Hospitals at three locations see advertising below   (250) 652-4312

10 Best of the Best, quick reference
Walks / Hikes

Botanical Beach, Port Renfrew	W1	page	68
China Beach, Juan de Fuca trail	W2		70
Cowichan River Footpath, Lake Cowichan	D2		90
Dallas Rd., Clover to Ogden Point, Victoria	V2		22
East Sooke Regional Park, East Sooke	W4		74
Monteque Provincial Park, Galiano Island	D10		106
Newcastle Island Prov. Park, Nanaimo	N1		108
Sidney Spit Provincial Marine Park	P8		58
Thetis Lake Regional Park, View Royal	V10		36
Witty's Lagoon Reg. Park, Metchosin	W8		82

Best Swimming Holes

Bright Angel Park, Duncan	fresh water	D3	page	92
Coles Bay Regional Park	ocean water	P7		56
Cowichan River Footpath	fresh water	D2		90
Durance Lake, Mount Work	fresh water	P4		50
Koksilah River	fresh water	D4		94
Little Qualicum Falls	fresh water	N3		114
Matheson Lake Reg. Park	fresh water	W6		78
North Beach, Beaver Lake	fresh water	P1		43
West Beach, Thetis Lake	fresh water	V10		36
Spectacle Lake, Malahat	fresh water	D7		100

128

50 BEST DOG-WALK/HIKES - INDEX-

Acknowledgements

Was it not for Jazz, our lovely golden retriever, I would never have had the idea to write this dog-walking/hiking guide.

Over the 12 years we have lived on Vancouver Island, Jazz's needs and abilities changed from a tireless running and fish-catching dog to a more sedate walker. With that we had to find new territory to suit her capacity for shorter walks. When we were hiking last spring, I noticed changes in regulations at several parks that caused familiar areas to be off-limits for us. It was time to bring order in a confusing state of "on and off leash" areas, newly-initiated parking fees and other matters.

I would like to thank B.C. Parks for confirming my collected data and use of some park maps. I also owe much gratitude to the CRD Parks for exact information and availability of clear maps. Wyeth Animal Health, Guelph Ont., allowed me to use the 'tick" identification card. Quotes in the introductory chapters came from 'Animal Blessings,' (ISBN 0-06-251645-0) a beautiful selection of writings honoring the animals we love.

Many people have supported and helped me in different ways to produce this final product. For prudent advice, I like to thank in particular Mrs. Melanie Groves, Communications Coordinator at CRD Parks Department in Victoria, Brian Farghuar, Manager CVRD Parks Department in Duncan and Dr. Patrick Benloulou, Jazz's veterinarian. Thanks go to my brother Jan, who had the splendid idea to rate the hikes with doggy bones. For effortless proofreading and corrections, I would like to thank Stephanie van Hoof and my writing tutor Michael Crawley.

At the production level, I thank the people at Trafford Publishing for their patience and understanding.
For encouragement, I would like to thank the many people I spoke to since inception of the book, but in particular my wife Marianne, friends Jorien and Frits Elbers, Joke and Cor Jonker, Eddy Muka and Peni Fitzpatrick and Georgia Virag.

Recommended reading:

Walking My Dog, Jane, by Ned Rozell

What about this for a walk; from Valdez to Prudhoe Bay along
the Trans-Alaska pipeline

Best Beaches and accessibility

Beach	Location Map	Page	Comments
Cadboro Bay Beach, East Saanich	V5	28	Fine all year, except one section is off limits after 9 a.m. from May – Aug.
China Beach, Juan de Fuca trail	W2	70	Dogs should be leashed
Cordova Spit, Saanichton	P9	60	Be courteous to the First Nations People
Island View Beach, Reg. Park, Saanichton	P10	62	Walking is fine all year, but dogs can not **stay** between June1 and Sept.15
Monteque Provincial Park, Galiano Island	D10	106	Dogs should be leashed
Newcastle Island, Prov. Park, Nanaimo	N1	108	Dogs should be leashed
Rathtrevor Prov. Park, Parksville	N2	112	No dogs in day-use area from March 15 to Oct. 15. Leashed everywhere else.
Sidney Spit Provincial Marine Park	P8	58	Dogs should be leashed
Willows Beach, Oak Bay	V3	24	No dogs allowed on the beach from May 1 to Sept. 30
Witty's Lagoon, Reg. Park, Metchosin	W8	82	No dogs on beach from June 1 to Sept. 15